BLACKLISTED IN
BHUTAN

Love Lost and Love Transformed in the
Land of Gross National Happiness

RIEKI CRINS

CONTENTS

MY STORY STARTS WITH AN ENDING

The ending of a very long relationship.

Of 27 years of love, and excitement, and hope, devotion, commitment and hard work, and then of betrayal and deep depression.

But first, there is the ending. And it's pretty bad, as endings go.

IN LIMBO

November 2016.

I was waiting in Bangkok.

I was used to waiting in Bangkok. Bangkok is where you wait for your visa to Bhutan.

Like so many times before, I had handed in my application at the Bhutanese embassy, and now I was waiting for approval.

This time, I was particularly excited. I was going to

visit our hotel school, the school near Paro town that I had set up and worked so hard to get funded. A long relationship was coming to fruition.

Our hotel school in Paro was an old run down hotel built in traditional Bhutanese style with the 10 lucky signs painted on the walls. We had rented the building on a rice field near the airport and renovated it to become a three star hotel, restaurant and school. Every year, forty students from disadvantaged backgrounds trained there to start a career in the hotel sector. They were learning to become chefs, food and beverage managers and housekeepers for five star hotels. This project was my ultimate labour of love. A vision of many years had become a reality.

Over the course of 27 years, Bhutan has been a large part of my life. I went there twice for extended periods of anthropological research, in 1990 and 2008 (for my MA and then my Ph.D). I also worked there regularly as a guide for high-end tourism from 1999 onwards, helping many Bhutanese organisations. The hotel school in Bhutan was the biggest project of my life. It took years of dedication and hard work.

Although I was the one who brought in all the

money, I never received any payment for my work. All the funds I was able to raise went into the creation of the school. And there it was. My beautiful school in Bhutan.

And here I was, waiting in a Bangkok hotel room on Sukhumvit road.

Although I love being in Bangkok, after a few days the heat, the traffic jams, the shopping malls and the city people became a bit too much for me. I was looking forward to the crisp mountain air, clear skies and beautiful views over the snow-capped mountains dotted with ancient monasteries in Bhutan. Even the four-hour flight has always been a joy to me. If the sky is clear, the view over the Himalaya mountain range is spectacular, and it is always fun to bump into Bhutanese people I know and haven't seen in a long time. On the previous flight I had met a friend who owned a hotel in Thimphu. He had gone to Bangkok to shop for a flat screen TV. These screens are very popular in Bhutan. At the Bangkok airport you can see many Bhutanese standing in line to check in, all with huge flat screen TVs, rice cookers and other items that are hard to get in Bhutan.

Throughout my years traveling to Paro, I often met famous people on the plane, like the writer Amy Tang or the actress Cameron Diaz, who was travelling to Bhutan to make an MTV video – she even stayed in the same hotel!

The flights from Bangkok to Bhutan are usually very early hour in the morning, but people are always willing to chat, which creates a friendly atmosphere.

My suitcase was packed, all my papers were in order. I had my flight ticket and the money that I needed to take to the school. I was brought a pasta machine and a waffle iron along for the students. I was excited about teaching the kids how to make Dutch waffles and Italian pasta. But right now I was waiting for an email from Mr Jigme, my Bhutanese partner for the hotel school.

Ping!! There it was, the message I was waiting for.

I opened my mail, and I couldn't believe what I was reading.

Mr Jigme wrote that my visa application had been rejected.

"What I have you done?" he asked.

I had done nothing. Except setting up a successful

hotel school in the country, spending the last two years helping 150 marginalised young people to train for a good job, and working without payment for a long time to get this project off the ground! That's what I'd done!

I grabbed my phone and called Mr Jigme. He picked up immediately.

"Mr Jigme, what's going on?"

"Oh Aum Rieki, I went to the immigration office today to get your visa, but they told me that you are blacklisted!"

Blacklisted! The word reverberated around my mind. I couldn't take it in.

"What have you done?" Mr Jigme insisted.

"Mr Jigme, I've done nothing except fundraising, working hard to support the school. What is this about?"

"Aum, they refused to tell me why you've been blacklisted. Are you sure you've done nothing wrong?"

I wracked my brain. It had never occurred to me before that I could have done anything wrong in Bhutan.

"No, Mr Jigme", I said, trying to keep calm because

I could hear my voice wobble a bit. "I can't think of anything. I'm not a spy, I'm not involved in politics, and I'm certainly not a criminal."

Mr Jigme couldn't think of anything either, he said.

But there must be something!

"The only thing I ever did is to help Bhutan and be good to your country," I repeated. Then my voice broke.

I put down the phone and sat down at the desk. My body started to shake. How could this possibly be true? So many years of hard work and dedication to the country and it ends like this?

Then the tears came. There I was, sitting in my Bangkok hotel room, looking out at the huge grey clouds of the rainy season, ready to burst open, and I cried.

Thoughts were racing through my mind. Who could have done this to me? Could there be some kind of jealousy because of the success of our hotel school? I couldn't puzzle it out.

The first person I needed to talk to was my

foundation board partner Paolo. His visa had already been issued.

Paolo arrived at my hotel in the evening. We went for dinner in a nice restaurant, and over a selection of delicious Thai food, I told him the bad news.

He couldn't believe it either. "It must be a mistake," he kept saying, "this is impossible. How can they do this?" Paolo is from a family of diplomats, so I thought if anyone could help me it would be him.

"I'll try to do my best to find out what's going on in Bhutan, and why they refused to give you a visa," he said. And, when my tears came back, he reassured me saying, "Don't worry, I'll see if I can fix this."

I wished him good luck, and we agreed to meet again in Bangkok two weeks later.

I decided to stay in Thailand. I thought I could use my time to visit friends and try to lobby the Bhutanese embassy in Bangkok. But that proved very difficult. I called them and wrote to them, but they just kept saying: "Your local counterpart has to deal with this."

The embassy worker I was talking to on the phone even told me: "You're the first person I know who didn't get a visa to go to Bhutan." That made me feel even more miserable.

I tried to stay strong, decided to have a lot of massages, catch up on my reading and eat a lot of the amazing street food until Paolo came back from Bhutan, and we could assess the whole situation.

Nobody knew what had happened.

But there it was: after 27 years, my relationship with Bhutan had been cut off.

I could not go back.

CHAPTER I

MY LOVE AFFAIR
WITH BHUTAN

Being blacklisted after a love affair of 27 years with Bhutan felt like a nasty divorce. Suddenly your long-term partner doesn't want you anymore. Suddenly it's over. End of story. And the nastiest thing is that they don't even tell you why. Things are changing in Bhutan, I thought. Maybe

Bhutan is no longer the country I once fell in love with.

My love affair started in a remote village in North West Bhutan, a 12-hour hike into the mountains from the "all weather" road. The name of this village is Tsachaphu, Hot Spring at the End of the Valley. In this village I experienced traditional Bhutanese life, unchanged for many centuries. The village was at the end of a valley in the midst of dense forests. At the bottom of the valley the *Po Chu* or Father River, a strong mountain stream, provided the rice terraces on the steep slopes with water, and traditional farm Bhutanese farm houses clustered on top of the hill.

FIRST ENCOUNTER

When the letter came I knew this was my chance. A rare chance for a Masters student from the Netherlands to experience real fieldwork in a place that was still untouched" by westernisation.

I held the letter in my hand and started to dream. I imagined stepping into the footsteps of the anthropologists from the early twentieth century who suffered hardships in Africa or a remote island in the Pacific.

But Bhutan? I had never heard of it! I referred to the Encyclopaedia Britannica (in those days, there was no access to the Internet) and found only a very brief description of Bhutan. The encyclopaedia stated that Bhutan is an absolute Buddhist monarchy in the Eastern Himalayas. I also learnt that the people there carried swords and that it was inhabited by bears. Rather than putting me off, this lack of information intrigued me. There clearly was still a lot to be discovered about Bhutan.

I wrote back to my professor and told him that I would love to take up the opportunity to visit Bhutan. Shortly afterwards, I was selected. Bhutan was going to happen. To me.

We were a team of six students, three anthropology students and three students studying irrigation technology, and also three women and three men.

Marleen, Anita and Dirk were engineering students who specialised in irrigation, and I soon realised they were "hardliners", used to conducting fieldwork in very remote places in Indonesia or the Philippines, and used to living in very Spartan conditions. Some of them had stayed in a mud hut in a remote village for months without any comfort, sleeping on the floor and eating only rice and chilli paste. Anita, especially, was very politically engaged and worried about the situation in Bhutan.

"Are we doing the right thing," she said, "to offer our help to this country that is an absolute kingdom, which means it is a dictatorship?"

I told her that there would not be many countries outside Europe that were politically correct. She had to agree.

"And besides", I said, "our six month stay won't have a big impact on the country, we are not important." The other two men, both anthropologists like me, were very different. Ian was a romantic, he was mostly interested in drinking tea with the king of Bhutan and fighting bears. He was nostalgic and wished he had been born 100 years earlier to be a high official in the British Raj. Ralf was especially interested in photography, he was the most mature and down to earth of us all.

We were invited to join a programme organised

by the Department of Agriculture of the Royal Government of Bhutan. The Bhutanese government needed information on how Bhutanese farmers grew crops, particularly rice, in order to facilitate the implementation of improvements in the agricultural sector and to find ways of increasing crop yield. We anthropologists needed to study the social organisation in the village and its effect on rice cultivation and irrigation. How did the villagers organise the whole process? How was the water management set up? How were the irrigation channels maintained? We also needed to know how the farmers organised the planting of the seedlings and the ploughing of the fields.

For the very first time, I was going to a research station in the field. It was unsettling. We didn't really have much to prepare because we didn't know what to expect. We assumed that Bhutan would look like Tibet, with towering mountains and lots of snow. So we tried to prepare for all kinds of weather but everything else was completely unknown. We had only heard that the meals and lodging provided would be very basic.

After a long journey by plane via New Delhi in India and Kathmandu in Nepal, we arrived in Paro, Bhutan, on a sunny day in February 1990.

Our small plane landed on a short landing strip between towering mountains. Paro International Airport consisted of one small building then, not much larger than a barn. The air was crisp and clean, and I felt as though I had landed in a fairy tale. We saw impressive buildings that almost looked like castles, surrounded by rice terraces. To me, the houses looked like Swiss chalets with Asian features. The city of Paro itself was mostly one line of old wooden buildings along a road, at the end of which was a gigantic fortress. To my inexperienced self, it all looked very oriental and very familiar at the same time. It reflected the mental image I had of Switzerland in the middle ages.

In Kathmandu airport we saw the first Bhutanese people: three men in what looked to me like colourful knee length skirts and two women in long straight dresses. Later we learned that the men were wearing a *gho*, the Bhutanese version of a Tibetan *chuba*, a bit like a knee length coat held together with a colourful rope. The women wore a garment called a *kira* that they draped around themselves, with a belt around the waist and two silver buckles, one on each shoulder. We stared at them because we were excited to see them. They looked very different from the Indians or the Nepalese.

We walked out of the plane into the wooden shack that was the arrival hall. Huge posters of the King of Bhutan looked down on us. I saw Anita's face and had to laugh.

I told her: "Yes girl, we are under his guidance for the next few months, better get used to it!" Outside the sun was shining and it was very warm but inside the shack it was very cold and there was a strange smell that would stay with me for the rest of my life. It was the scent of freshly cut pinewood mixed oddly with the stench of rotten meat. At the time I didn't know what it was, but I later found out that this was the smell of betel nut, the smell that defines Bhutan.

The immigration officers were very friendly, their big smiles revealed red teeth and a welcome to Bhutan.

"It looks so nice when people wear traditional clothes instead of the boring western suits or uniforms," I told Marleen.

We got our passports stamped and went to pick up our bags from the landing strip. Outside the airport, two officials from the ministry of agriculture were waiting for us in front of their four-wheel drive Toyota Hiluxes and drove us to Thimphu, the capital of Bhutan.

Our driver was very proud of his car and the highway that connected the country from West to East, the only road in the country then. To us, it seemed like a narrow track, something you might see in remote villages in Europe. But looking at the massive mountains around us, we started to get an idea of how difficult it must have been to build this road.

The drive to Thimphu was breath taking. We were surrounded by dramatic mountain scenery, and here and there we could see beautiful white buildings with a red line painted around them. "These are monasteries and temples," our driver explained. I realised there were so many, some very small, some big, but all very rustic and picturesque. We were very quiet in the car, all occupied with our own thoughts. I realised how special it was to be here, just driving down that road.

"It's karma that brought you here," said our driver, "you must have been Bhutanese in your previous life, otherwise you would not be here." We all looked at each other, could this be true? "You know we don't let many foreigners in, so you are special."

Wow! It was a lot to take in.

After four hours of a roller coaster drive - we were all car sick, that mountain road didn't run in a straight line for more than a few metres at a time - we approached the capital Thimphu.

Thimphu looked like a small village to us. No traffic lights or commercial billboards. Again, my point of reference was an Asian version of an ancient Alpine settlement. The main road was a long stretch of pretty wooden shops, and at the end of the road the big *dzong* (a fortress from the sixteenth century) and many temples and monasteries looked down on us. Our driver pointed out that this was also where the government building was, next to a nine-hole golf course that belonged to the king. In the outskirts, a new part of town was under construction, mainly modern Indian style apartments for the growing population of Thimphu.

The Bhutanese government had rented an apartment for us in this part of town, in a big ugly concrete building. Almost immediately, and perhaps predictably for a young woman from Northern Europe, I started to worry about hygiene. Although the house was relatively new, the stairways were very dirty and there were red stains everywhere that looked like spit, and again I could smell that weird scent like rotten meat. Many dogs roamed around the building.

Our apartment was big, cold and empty, with only a table, chairs and a stove in the middle of the room. There was a basic kitchen and three bedrooms with six beds. All the windows had iron bars and our view was onto a square with a petrol station. Not the best view!

This apartment was where we would live for the first week of our stay in Bhutan, while we would be briefed about our research. We tried to make our "new home" a bit cosier by sticking posters and prayer flags up on the walls. The kitchen had a big concrete sink with a gas cooker and a water filter. We needed to boil the water and then filter it. We also had a small fridge.

We noticed that the air was crisp and thin. Timphu is high up in the mountains. In February it was still winter and very cold, and we were very grateful for the wood burning stove called *bukari* in our living room. Dirk liked to make a big fire, and one night the *bukari* was so hot that the wooden floor around it burst into flames. We thought that was hilarious and teased Dirk about it for some time.

Dirk turned out to be a bit eccentric. He was the first of us to buy a *gho* and wear it day and night. He loved being in Bhutan and adjusted very quickly to the new lifestyle. I could see he had the ambition of being as much like the locals as possible. I, on the other hand, struggled with being in Bhutan at first. Although I realised it was a big adventure I also was kind of homesick. Just before I left for Bhutan I had fallen in love and I missed my boyfriend so much. He had promised to wait for me but it was a very inconvenient moment to start a new relationship! On the other hand, I also saw it as a test to find out if the relationship would last. Marleen had the same problem, only she had known her boyfriend a bit longer. The fact that there was no phone or any other quick means of communication with the outside world didn't make it easier to cope with my situation.

But there was a lot distraction from my pining heart just by having to cope with the new situation. Being with the group was a lot of fun. We shared a sense of humour and we laughed a lot

Practical daily life was something to get used to. Because of the altitude, it took forever to boil water for tea. There were frequent power cuts and we had to use candles for light. There was only one shop in Thimphu selling a very few Western products, called shop Number Seven. There you could get things like peanut butter, laundry detergent, shampoo, toothpaste, chocolate and cookies. Most of the items were out of date and the cookies tasted like mildew. The chocolate had a white film on it but to us it was a treat and we made the best of it, particularly when we learned that from now on our diet would be rice with melted cottage cheese, and chillies, of course, lots of chillies. Bhutanese people love chillies and eat them in large quantities. A special delicacy, we were told, was dried pork, especially the fatty part with skin attached and that, of course, was soaked in chilli oil too!

Our stay in Thimphu was a good first introduction to Bhutanese lifestyle. Because Bhutanese people were not yet used to seeing *chillips* (white foreigners), everyone was very interested in us wherever we went. So interested, that they came to visit us in our apartment day and night. Often in the morning when I woke up and went into the living room, a few monks were sitting right next to the stove. Nobody knew who they were and where they came from. We couldn't talk to them because we didn't speak the language, and there was no dictionary of *dzongkha*. Our door was open and people just came in to be with us and to check us out. That weeklong training on the do's and don'ts of Bhutanese society, provided by the government, was very useful. We had the opportunity to learn a lot. If we had wanted to, we could have qualified for a driver's license for a steamroller! Very useful. And even a license to drive a steam train engine – particularly useful, we thought, in a country where there are no trains, but we didn't say that aloud. We also learned not to wear black clothes because they attract evil spirits, and we learned that everything in Bhutanese society involved astrology and spirits, in addition to the official Buddhist religion. We would soon find out this affected daily life.

Dirk and Ian were going to be sent to a village in East Bhutan, and Rolf and Anita to South Bhutan. Marleen and I would go to a village named Tsachaphu, the place that became my first Bhutanese true love. Ours was the most difficult posting because the village was a day's walk from the town of Punakha. It had no access road and could only be reached by foot and/or on horseback.

CHAPTER 2

TSACHAPHU, A VILLAGE AT THE END OF A VALLEY

Finally, the day we had to leave for our posting arrived. For four hours, we drove from Thimphu to Punakha, again in a Toyota High Lux provided by the Department of Agriculture. We realised how few cars there were on the road. Most of the vehicles we saw were four-wheel drive vehicles, and they all belonged to the Bhutanese government. A few smaller Indian jeeps were used as shared taxis. It seemed that most people walked everywhere.

To reach Punakha, we had to drive over a pass at an altitude of 3,200 metres with a spectacular view of the Eastern Himalayan mountain range. This was the *Dochu La*. Mountain passes are sacred because of the high altitude, where you come close to the gods. Every mountain pass has *stupas* (a dome-shaped building erected as a Buddhist shrine) and attached to the stupas are hundreds of colourful prayer flags. That first time, a heavy mist blanketed the pass, giving it a gloomy and mysterious atmosphere. You could imagine spirits and other transcendental creatures in the air. But when the mist lifted, a spectacular panorama became visible, with snow-capped mountains all the way to Tibet.

Maybe it was in that moment that I my heart opened to Bhutan.

It was very cold on the pass, and we kept on driving. Slowly, we came down to a lower altitude again, and the vegetation was slowly changing from high mountain forests to subtropical banana trees, orange trees and many kinds of ferns. Closer to Punakha we saw many rice fields. The driver told us that Punakha was a very fertile valley.

We needed a pit stop but realised there was no toilet close to the road and no restaurant either. Of course, even if there had been a restaurant, it would not have had a toilet anyway because in those days people just relieved themselves outside behind a tree. We had to get used to this because from now on there would be no more toilets! I only realised this later.

During the final leg of our journey, we passed through rice terraces and a dry riverbed. The car stopped at a wooden shack that served as a store. Some men were already waiting for us there. I wondered how they had received the information, since there was no phone. The driver advised us to buy basic supplies in the shack that was a store and a bar and restaurant. Restaurant is a generous description. There was a rough table with two benches inside, and we could buy some instant noodle soup. That was the only dish they had. We bought a big supply of dried chillies, tea, candles, kerosene and betel nuts. Now I know why most Bhutanese have red teeth and where the smell comes from. It is from betel nuts. Many Bhutanese are addicted to it and it is so bad that many older people, both men and women, have red mouths with a few red stained rotten teeth inside. "How do they kiss?" I asked Marleen. Marleen looked at me and said: "Uuhhh, I can't imagine kissing a stained mouth like that." Maybe they don't kiss at all," I said.

The men waiting for us helped us carry our luggage up the mountain on small sturdy horses. I had bought a light mattress in Thimphu because I was told that in the villages people sleep on the wooden floor. I didn't want to sleep on a hard floor for six months, so I carried that mattress with me, a little bit of luxury! The mattress was made of natural rubber and very soft, it was not hard for a small mountain horse to carry on its back. We also took food, kerosene, candles and, of course, our backpacks. We also brought gifts for the villagers, such as dried chillies, tea and betel nuts.

We set off with the men and the small horses, following the *Po Chu*, or Father River, up the mountain. The landscape was spectacularly beautiful. It seemed as though I was travelling through three climate zones and three seasons in a day. If I looked skywards, I could see snow-capped mountains. I was walking along a path lined with trees in autumn colours. After a few hundred metres, I found myself in a tropical microclimate with big, beautiful blue butterflies and orchids, where the sun shone bright and warm.

From Punakha to Tsachaphu, the path climbed about 1,000 metres. Marleen and I didn't talk much, we were both struggling to keep up with the porters who walked on their bare feet. Their gait was so light and easy, they almost floated. Marleen and I with our high tech hiking boots struggled along. We had to cross mountain streams, rice fields and dense forests. The path was not very clear and sometimes we just stumbled on roots and boulders that we couldn't see. The biodiversity that surrounded us was stunning. On the lower level we walked along the river and cute otters were playing in the water, they were not afraid of us at all. When I walked very close to them, they just looked up and played on. As the path wound up and down, we walked over harvested rice fields and then entered a tropical forest again. After climbing up for another hour, the landscape changed back to the pinewoods we had left behind at the mountain pass. I wondered about the animals that must live here. Later on I learned that bears, cobras, wild boars, barking deer and many others were part of this wild landscape.

But in spite of all the spectacular nature, Marleen and I were getting seriously exhausted from the long, arduous walk. At one point, I felt like giving up, thinking, I cannot go further. I feel dead. At that very moment, one of the men pointed out the village in the distance. But although it looked very close, we still had to hike an hour before getting there.

From the distance, the village looked beautiful, almost a fairy tale setting. A handful of houses dotted the mountainside, surrounded by rice fields, all nestled above the Po Chu river.

And then we arrived, tired and covered in sweat, in the village we were going to stay in for six months. We walked down the small path between a few houses, and there it was. The house I was going to spend the next six months in!

But when I got a closer view the house I was going to live in, I wanted to cry. From a distance, it had looked nice and well kept, but close up it was a very different story.

"Marleen, can you imagine that we have to live here for the next six months?"

"Yes," said Marleen, "this is normal. Most places we are sent to have living conditions like this." I had travelled a lot in Asia and Africa, but when travelling I could choose the places I stayed. I never really appreciated what it would mean to actually live in basic conditions with no twentieth century comforts for such a long time.

"I think I made a mistake!" I told Marleen.

The house was a typical traditional Bhutanese house. The bull, the cows and the pigs lived on the ground floor. You had to climb a wooden ladder carved out of a tree trunk to get to the human living quarters, consisting of two rooms, one for living, cooking, eating and sleeping, and one for storage. No electricity, no plumbing, no chairs or tables. The storage room would be my new home for the coming months. Marleen would stay with a different family, a 20-minute walk from my house. My landlady climbed down the tree trunk ladder and invited us into her home. It was quite impressive to see how many villagers managed to gather so quickly to see what was going on.

I would have loved a hot shower and a cold drink, preferably an ice-cold beer, after that long walk. My landlady offered me butter tea instead, a Tibetan style black tea with salt, a pinch of soda and butter that tastes more like soup than tea. Well, I thought, I'll just have to adjust to this way of life. After all, this is why I came to Bhutan.

So from now on, my toilet was outside in the bushes and my washroom was outside at a tap. At first, the whole village would come to take a peek at me, while I was soaping my body with a sarong rapped around me. So Marleen and I decided to go into the forest to wash ourselves in a mountain stream. But even this was complicated because in the vicinity of a Bhutanese village, you are never alone, even deep in the forest. And in addition, the forest was full of leeches trying to attach themselves to us.

I also noticed that everybody was wearing very dirty clothes and my landlady was very dirty except for her face. I learned later that there was a good reason for this, and washing is something for people in modern houses. I had to adjust to this too.

My landlady was called Aum Zam. I noticed quickly that she was not as easy to get along with as many of the other villagers. At this time, in 1990, Aum Zam, must have been around 55 years old. In the village however age was always a rough estimate. The villagers didn't know how old they were because children were not registered at birth, or indeed at any time. Aum Zam must once have been very beautiful, actually she still was, but she had a huge goitre. Many older women had this problem here, and I learned later that it was due to iodine deficiency. Her neck was darkened with dirt and so were her clothes. You could hardly see the colour of her kira. I don't think she ever had a bath in her life. Her clothes had never been washed. This was normal in the village. People lived very close to nature and their domestic animals, like the cows and bulls, pigs and chickens that lived on our ground floor. A few hundred years ago, this was commonplace in Europe, too. And I quickly discovered one reason, at least, for not washing too often. The dirt served as a protective layer against bites from bugs, lice and other insects. I learned this the hard way, because all kind of bugs feasted on me and my freshly washed skin.

THE STORY OF AUM ZAM

Aum Zam had three sons, all three from different fathers. Although I couldn't talk to her, I understood that one son, Nala, her youngest, was a monk and lived in the *dzong*, a big monastery in Punakha. Her two other sons lived with her in our house, all of them in the one main room, and helped her on the farm. Aum Zam was a very religious woman and she was an *ngejum* (female shaman). She could tell the future by reading rice and go into a trance to talk to her spirit deity. In the village, all farmers had cattle. To feed the cattle, men and women would take the cows into the forest for days, sometimes for weeks. And sometimes a cow got lost in the woods. It was hard to track down the lost cow, but cows were very valuable. So people came to consult Aum Zam on where to look for the cow. Aum Zam would sit outside with a basket of rice grains, concentrating on the rice, then put her hand into the basket and moved the rice around in various different directions. She was mumbling mantras and prayers and after a while she told the farmer where to look in the forest. It seemed to work because the farmers never came back to complain that the prediction was not accurate.

As a true villager of her time, Aum Zam had no idea about money. I paid her money for staying in her house but she would have preferred it if I had paid her in kind, in chillies, cheese, betel nuts, or tea. She would tell me: "I can't eat money!" And I could see her point. There were no shops in the village.

My first weeks at Aum Zam's house were very tough. Although my adventure in the village was a long-time dream that was now becoming reality, it took me quite some time to adjust. I think I had culture shock. I felt disoriented, as if I'd had been sent back a few hundred years in time. My watch, Walkman and small transistor radio were the only objects from modern industrialised society, and they became very dear to me. I was lucky that I had thought to bring a large supply of batteries.

My room was Aum Zam's storage room where she

kept there her rice, dried meat and many containers with a local alcohol called *arra*. The villagers had constructed a small platform for me, so I didn't have to sleep on the floor. I was very happy that I had brought my mattress with me, a little comfort. There was also a folding table and two chairs, supplied by the government for us. Nobody in the village had a chair, or a table or a bed and mattress. People sat on the floor and slept on the floor. A bamboo wall divided my room from the main room, where Aum Zam and her two sons slept. At night I had many rats in my room. Sometimes they would run over me. There was not much that I could do, I just hoped Aum Zam's cat would eat them. When that didn't happen, or maybe there were just too many of them, I tried to imagine they weren't there. I had a kerosene stove too, at least I could boil my water. I had brought the kerosene with me all the way on the little horses.

During the first weeks I joined Aum Zam and her family in all their meals. Aum Zam had an adobe stove in the main room fuelled by wood collected in the forest by her sons. This was where she cooked her rice. Next to the stove was a huge earthen pot in which she kept water. Village cooking was very easy and didn't take much effort. The staple food was local red rice, eaten with *tsum,* a sauce made from cheese, any kind of vegetable, and chillies, all cooked together. We always had butter tea with our food, as we had on the day of my arrival. Breakfast, lunch and dinner were the same.

In the beginning, when Aum Zam called me for breakfast, I got out of my bed, put some clothes on and didn't bother to wash because I thought I knew that no one washed themselves. I walked into Aum Zam's room to sit down on the floor for breakfast with my plate and spoon. But Aum Zam started to scream at me, and slowly I realised that there was an exception to the no-wash custom. She was scolding me because it was unacceptable to eat before you washed your face. This also explained why she herself had such a clean face.

At every meal, we would sit down in a circle, around a bowl of rice in the middle, and some *ezay,* a homemade chilli paste, very hot and pungent. And there was butter tea, of course.

Everyone had their own bamboo basket and a

wooden cup for the tea and *tsum*. We all ate with our hands. We cleaned them afterwards by rubbing a few grains of cooked rice together in our palms. After the meal, we all licked our bamboo basket and cups clean and that was that. No washing up except for the cooking pots. I hadn't anticipated how little cleaning and housekeeping needed to be done here. The traditional Bhutanese clothes turned out to be very practical. The *kira* and *gho* were made in such a way that they could also be used as bedding, so no mattress or sheets were necessary. At bed time, Aum Zam and her sons just lay down on the floor and covered themselves with their clothes.

I also had to get used to the smoke in the room. The stoves in the farmhouses didn't have chimneys, so the smoke was everywhere and sometimes my eyes burned. I could see that everything in the house was covered in soot.

"This cannot be healthy," I told Marleen.

"I think it also has a practical reason," she replied, "the soot covers the beams to protect them against insects and the smoke cures the meat they put above the stove." I thought that was a good explanation. But many villagers had eye infections due to the smoke in their houses.

Every morning I woke up to the screaming voice of Aum Zam: "Pangeh, Namgeh, lho sa - get up." This was the start of our day. Aum Zam would then start to cook breakfast and Namgeh and Pangeh didn't want to get up, so Aum Zam kept on screaming until they finally did.

In spite of that, I always loved the early mornings in the village. Every household would start burning incense to "clean" the house from the evil spirits of the night. It was such a beautiful ritual. After breakfast, the daily chores would be done and then Aum Zam fed the pigs and all the other animals downstairs.

CHAPTER 3

CELEBRATING LIFE, THE BHUTANESE WAY

I n the village all the days seemed alike to me. I realised that, coming from the West, I was accustomed to many ways of defining times and days and differentiating between them. All my life there had been weekends, different food every day, different clothes. In the village, every day of the week was the same, people ate the same food three times a day, every day, rice and chillies. And of course they wore the same clothes.

As I started to receive letters from home, I noticed that friends were asking me: "What are you doing at the weekend?" I had to laugh. There was no weekend. We didn't need to dress up. We didn't cook special food. We didn't go out.

The only special days in village life were the

religious festivals. February and March were the months when the villagers celebrated their annual *choku* or rituals to appease the local spirits and deities to secure a fertile rice crop. Marleen and I were invited to all these occasions.

Our first invitation came from a wealthy family. This family had lots of land, a big house and a very elaborate altar room full of Buddha figures, ancient old scriptures and silver bowls with water offerings and huge phallus symbols made out of rice (called *thormas*). Marleen and I arrived in the early morning. We had our plates and cups with us. Tsachaphu, our village, was a collection of buildings spread over a big area. We were living in the hamlets of Neptenka and Dengana, both near the top of the mountainside. Phub Dorji's house was at the bottom of the mountain, next to the river. So we had to climb down many levels of rice fields to get there.

We arrived at the house and our host greeted us with a big smile. I could feel he was very happy that we were there. He immediately offered us *arra,* a strong homemade rice wine. We had been told that we should refuse three times when people offered us something as a polite gesture. But then you also had to accept three times! So my big mug was filled to the brim with *arra*, and I had to drink it in one gulp. And that three times!

Marleen was struggling with it too. It was early morning, and we both hadn't eaten that much, so the inevitable result was that we became quite drunk, very quickly.

Inside the house, there were a lot of monks, praying, banging on drums and blowing on long horns that remind me of Swiss alphorns. Some people were sitting on the floor and eating, others walked around, and even small children were drinking *arra* and smoking cigarettes.

"Do you see all these children behaving like adults," Marleen said. "Yes," I told her, "I think in this culture they think what is 'good' for adults is also 'good' for children."

Phub Dorji could speak a bit of English, and he saw that I was very friendly with the children. He came to next to me and said: 'Do you like Bhutanese children?" "Yes," I said.

He asked, "Why don't you try me then?"

Wow! That was a very straightforward offer!

I have to admit that Phub Dorji was a very handsome man. And even after a few days in the village, I had noticed how kind the men were to children and how much they helped around the house. But I was still longing for my love at home and therefore not very interested in a new boyfriend. Every day, I was waiting for a love letter. I also wrote long letters to him.

Because Phub Dorji's family was rich, he had a big house, twice the size of Aum Zam's. He also had a lot of land, many pigs and cows. In the village, you could tell if a family was rich by the amount of butter in the tea. The more butter swimming in the tea, the richer the family was.

Because of his wealth, Phub Dorji could afford a three day *choku* and all the villagers were invited. But as I looked around, I couldn't see Aum Zam. It seemed as if she was the only villager who was absent. Only her son Namgeh was there. But because of the language barrier, and because I didn't have a translator, I couldn't figure out what was going on.

There was hustle and bustle in the house, people coming and going. Women were cooking food on the adobe stove in huge pots. One girl was churning the butter tea in a large wooden pipe. To me, it looked like an old fashioned butter churner.

Phub Dorji offered us all the delicacies Tsachaphu had to offer: rich butter tea, red rice, lots of *tsum* and the piece the resistance: a big piece of pig fat with the skin and hair still attached to and red arteries that were clearly visible. It also smelled as if it was already a little rotten. Phub Dorji put it on my plate with a big smile.

"Oh my God, how can I refuse this?" I told Marleen. "Why don't we tell him we are vegetarians?" she said.

This is the solution, I thought. From now on we are vegetarian!

I explained to Phub Dorji with many gestures that we did not eat meat. This was absolutely acceptable and nobody lost face.

At Phub Dorji's house, witnessing the religious festival, I realised that I had landed in a medieval scene. All the guests were sitting in a large circle in the lotus position, their mouths stained red from betel nut chewing. Their clothes were all in various shades of brown, since they had all accumulated protective dirt. Dogs were roaming around and licked the pieces of food off the floor that people had spit out. After a while, some man and women were so drunk that they had to lie down in the corners of the room, sleeping their drunkenness off. Small children with no diapers on were crawling around, and one of the children had diarrhoea! But the dogs cleaned it all up. In the middle of this people were eating and chatting. Three monks were humming their mantras in the background and sometimes one of them fell asleep. Women walked around with huge vessels to serve people rice, butter tea, meat, *tsum* and lots of betel nuts. It reminded me of a Breughel painting.

Phub Dorji poured us more and more *arra*. I tried to refuse, but it was impossible. After a while one of the guests started to sing. My neighbour gestured to me that I had to sing a song too, from my country. The only song I could think of was "Summertime", so I sang the song and people liked it. Following that afternoon this song haunted me for the rest of my stay.

At the end of the day, before it got dark, I told Marleen: "We need to go home, we have to climb all the way up the mountain and we're so drunk it won't be easy."

"Why don't we stay here for the night?" Marleen said.

Even in my drunken condition, I had to say no. I was afraid the monks and all the drinking would go on all night and sleep would be difficult. I felt it was better to climb up the hill and get home.

So Marleen and I decided to scramble up the mountainside. I can remember pulling myself up the shelves of the rice terraces in a drunken haze, leaving the river behind far, far down the slope. But I made it.

I climbed up the tree ladder and crawled cautiously across the main room. When I opened the door to my bedroom I felt something big and wet hitting me in the face. In my drunken state I thought it must be an illusion. I managed to crawl a little further and into bed where I fell into a deep, alcohol-infused sleep. But in the middle of the night a horrible stench woke me up. I wanted to throw up.

Where did it come from? A sweet rotten smell filled the small room. I had never smelled anything so horrid and pungent in my life before. Even the worst sewage was nothing compared to this! I quickly ran out, slid down the tree ladder and finally couldn't help it anymore and threw up. When I made it back, still very unsteady on my feet, I used my flashlight to take a look around the room, to see where this stench came from. And I saw what I had felt last night on my face, wet and clinging to my skin. My room was filled with pieces of meat hanging from the ceiling on wooden poles, long strips of raw and rotting meat! This was what had hit me in the face last night. Aum Zam must have killed an animal and this was the way she tried to cure her meat. But Tshachapu is on an altitude that is too low to cure meat properly. It is too warm and too humid, and the meat starts to rot very quickly.

That stench again! It crept from my nostrils into my mouth. I felt sick again and had a huge hangover. I really couldn't stay in that room one minute longer. I decided to walk to Marleen's house, hoping to stay with her host family for a while.

MARLEEN AND MARRIAGE

Marleen lived with a family about a 20 minute walk away, in a small house that belonged to Namgeh Bida and her "husband" Namgeh. Namgeh was a young man of around 25, and he was "married" to Namgeh Bida. In Bhutan, marriage was a different concept from the one I was used to. Couples who slept with each other thought of themselves as "married" and the man most of the time moved in with the family of the girl. I couldn't help thinking that this was in sharp contrast to other countries in South Asia. In India and Nepal, the girl almost always leaves her home to live with the family of her husband and often the family of the girl has to give her husband's family a dowry that can be very costly. This is not the case in Bhutan. And in the village the gender equality was quite remarkable.

Marleen's room was very basic. She only had a sleeping bag and some personal items. Her room also had a big window open to the elements, with only a wooden shutter. So it was very cold in her room, and she had no heating. Marleen's host family rented this room out to earn income.

Mr Namgeh could speak a few words of English, and in the beginning it was helpful to talk to him. He helped us to understand a little bit of what was going on in the village. The three of us would walk far into forest and study the rice fields. Marleen needed to measure rainfall, the dimensions and locations of the fields and other agricultural data.

Namgeh told us that recently the *gup* (the village headman) had asked all the villagers to try to grow a new rice seed. This rice seed was called "miracle seed" and with it you could grow rice crops three times a year instead of once! But Namgeh also told us this rice needed a lot of "medicine" because it couldn't grow by itself or with the help of cow dung. By "medicine" Namgeh meant chemical fertiliser and all kinds of pesticides!

What was going on here? In the early 90s we knew that organic farming was the way forward. These people had been farming for hundreds of years in their own traditional way, why would they risk such a big change?

I asked Namgeh what the people in the village thought of this.

"No one wants to grow this rice," he told me. "It doesn't taste good and gives us heartburn. Also we have to buy all kinds of "medicine" and we have no money. Our red rice tastes much better, and we can put our cow dung on the fields."

After a few nights I moved back to Aum Zam's house. The meat had been removed from my room, but I don't know where it was stored.

BECOMING A VILLAGER

During the first month of our stay, Marleen and I needed to adjust. I was very happy that Marleen was there too because I was suffering from major culture shock. I was so homesick, sometimes I would hide behind a tree and cry my eyes out. I needed to hide somewhere because I had no privacy in my house or in the village. One day I was crying in the shelter of a tree, and I didn't even realise I was sitting next to a sleeping cobra! There were so many cobras in the rice fields, they had created huge caves as tall as a human, and there they spent the winter.

Marleen and I spent a lot of time together. We could talk about everything.

Marleen's living situation was difficult, too, and in a very different way from mine. Because we spent so much time with Namgeh, his wife Namgeh Bida became very jealous. So jealous that one day she gave Marleen old rice cakes for dinner that were normally used as temple offerings. Dry hard rice cakes full of bugs and fly droppings! I told Marleen: "It's time to move, you cannot stay there anymore. This is getting out of hand!"

Namgeh was from a village on the other side of the *Po Chu*, the Father River. He was from a very poor family and it would have been very difficult for him to go back to his mother. It would have been a huge loss of face, and he told us he loved Namgeh Bida and wanted to stay with her. So I thought it would be better if Marleen moved out so peace could be restored.

I also I had my problems with Aum Zam. I began to notice that people in the village felt sorry for me that I had to live with her. They constantly gossiped about her and she never attended the big religious rituals, although everybody else from the village was there. I already noticed that at Phub Dorji's house *choku*.

At first I was puzzled. Aum Zam was a very religious woman. My presence in her house was disturbing to her because I made so many mistakes. I offended the deities every day by doing things that were not good, like killing bugs. Once I was sitting close to the stove, it was evening and very cold outside, I was staring into the fire, feeling comfortable and warm. Suddenly a huge bug crept onto me. Reflexively I killed the bug. Aum Zam saw this and was shocked. She started to scream at me. I understood she was very upset about me killing a bug. As a good Buddhist she would never do that.

The next day, I threw paper into the fire on her stove. This was also a major mistake. By doing so I had offended the fire god. Every morning I wiped the floor of my room clean, and used the brush to throw the dirt outside. Again, Aum Zam started to scream at me. It was not an auspicious day to do that. It was also a taboo to whistle in the house, to step over a pan with rice, or sit on a pillow that was for your head because the head is considered sacred.

One day I became ill and had so much pain in my legs that I couldn't walk anymore. The neighbours said I was ill because of the evil eye. Apparently, Aum Zam was the intended target of that "evil eye", but because she was an *ngejum* she could protect herself from evil and she redirected it to me. The village monk came to my room to do a *puja* (ritual) to drive away the evil spirits who made me ill. I was lying in bed, feeling sick and scared, and the village monk came in with a hand drum and started to sing mantras and bang the drum above my head. I already had a massive headache so this was not helping. But I was very touched by the help from the village and that the monk tried to heal me. And I have to say that a day later I felt much better.

The spirituality and the magic in the village was everywhere, but I decided just to be an outside observer – if I could! Because I was in such a strange and alien environment, and didn't know much about Buddhism and animism, I decided to look at it with scientific, Western detachment. I had learned as an anthropologist that magic usually has an important function in a traditional society. It keeps harmony between people and their environment and creates meaning. Everything that happens has a purpose that is often hidden from the outsider.

I was content with the situation, but Aum Zam

seemed to suffer because of my ignorance. I disturbed so many deities in her house, it was a lot of work for her to perform the rituals and prayers necessary to restore the balance.

HOW TO LOSE YOUR TRANSLATORS

One morning there was a knock at my door. That was strange because usually nobody knocked and villagers just came in. Even at night, neighbours would come in to fetch a cigarette or anything they fancied, although I was asleep in my bed. In the beginning I had all my things laid out on a trunk that was my cupboard, but I learned quickly not to do that anymore because everyone who came to visit me took some of my things and never gave them back.

Children took my toothpaste and ate it as candy. Sometimes I saw little Tsering walking outside, and his *gho* (there is a very handy pouch in the gho that can be used as a pocket) showed a huge bulk at his belly. I saw that it was filled with my things. I said: "little thief, give me back my things!" Then I learned that things that are "out there", meaning not locked up inside a trunk, belong to everyone. From that moment on, I also locked up my personal property and only put communal things on my table and trunk.

So when I heard someone knocking, I was very curious.

"Come in," I said, and a handsome and cheeky young man came in. "I am Thinley and I come here to be your translator," he said. This was such good news, for many reasons, not least because the situation with Namgeh and Marleen was becoming too complex and his English was no longer sufficient for our research purposes.

"Who sent you", I said to Thinley. "The ministry of agriculture," he said. "I am here to help you guys." "Oh, you are very welcome."

"Thinley, where are you from?" "I am from Punakha," he said, "and I just finished high school, so now I am looking for a job, and I love to work with foreigners." His English sounded good.

So with Thinley here now, and Marleen's difficult situation, we needed a new place where Marleen and Thinley could stay. But it turned out that not many households in Tshachapu had a spare room. So we really needed to be creative and we decided to go to the village headman to ask him if he knew anyone who could rent out a room for Marleen.

The *gup* or village headman lived a few hours by foot from Tsachaphu. He was a rich man and owned a lot of land. He was respected by the villagers. Thinley told us that village headmen were chosen because they had to be very generous and wise. According to the villagers this *gup* was generous and wise.

He welcomed us warmly. We were served sweet tea which was a very welcome change after all the salty butter tea, and fresh cookies, so delicious! I had to control myself to avoid eating the whole plate at once because I hadn't eaten any food like this for such a long time.

The *gup* told us to talk to Mr Phurba who had a house with a bit of space on the second floor. According to the *gup*, Phurba was a very friendly man but he was deaf as a result of meningitis.

Mr. Phurba's home had been newly built. Under the roof there was space for Marleen and Thinley to move in. The room had a stove and finally Marleen had some privacy. It was also much closer to my house. I decided that, in spite of the wet rotten meat experience, I wanted to stay at Aum Zam's place because I had actually become quite comfortable there, and it also had become my office, with two chairs and a table.

Somehow, the village snuck up on me and given me a feeling of home.

So now we had a translator and we could actually talk to the villagers. We were excited. But then we ran into the next problem. Thinley didn't really translate our questions properly, and most of the time when I asked him to explain something and translate the answers, he would just say "Bhutanese custom". That didn't help much.

One day we were invited to a celebration in a house that belonged to three sisters, well known all over the village. The three sisters were building a new house and before the roof was raised, a big celebration was held. All the villagers were invited except, again, Aum Zam. During the celebrations I saw the women sitting on one side of the house and men on the other side. I saw that the three sisters had also invited all the carpenters and workmen who had built the new house, but what was very strange was that one carpenter was dressed like a woman and behaved like a woman, the whole day! When I asked Thinley why this was, his reply was, predictably: "Bhutanese custom!" Marleen and I were really puzzled by it.

Marleen's landlord Phurba was also at the party and he got very drunk. I saw him arguing with another man and then, suddenly, Phurba took out his knife (all men in the village wore big knives as everyday tools) and started to attack the guy. Blood spilled out everywhere. Marleen and I were in shock and the women dropped their drinks. Several men jumped on Phurba and restrained him. They took him aside and told him to lie down to sleep off his drunkenness. His victim was taken to another corner of the room with a dirty cloth on his wounds to stop the bleeding. And then we all went back to the celebrations as if nothing had happened.

The next day we went to Phurba to ask him what was this all about. He told us his side of the story through Thinley (this time he was willing to translate). Because Phurba was deaf, he always thought people were talking behind his back. And that afternoon during the celebrations, Phurba had destroyed the new water outlet in the village. A year ago, UNICEF Bhutan had come to the village and constructed a fresh water supply there. From then on, the villagers wouldn't have to go into the forest to collect water. But UNICEF had chosen the location and the dates of construction without consulting the astrologer. Soon after the tap was built, two people in the village got meningitis, and one of them was Phurba. He lost his hearing, and he nearly died. And so, when he felt strong enough, he destroyed the new water supply. Lu, the goddess of water, was disturbed and there had been no proper ritual to appease her. In Phurba's mind, that was the reason why he and others got sick.

After a week or so Thinley lost interest in working with us and told us he wanted to go home for a short holiday. He promised to come back in a few days but I was afraid he would stay away. However, to my surprise, Thinley came back after a few days, and he had some astonishing news about my landlady, Aum Zam. I knew that Aum Zam had three sons, two who lived here with us, and another one called Nala who was a monk. Thinley had seen Nala in the *dzong* in Punakha and he had noticed that Nala was standing in a special section of the *dzong* reserved for monks, who were descended from slaves.

So Thinley had found out that Aum Zam belonged to the Zap caste, a former slave caste. In the past, she was the personal slave of a high lama. After the abolishment of slavery in 1958, the government gave slaves and the descendants of slaves land and a house, and this was how Aum Zam ended up in Tsachaphu. The King of Bhutan had given her land in this village. But it seemed that she was still stigmatised, and this was why she was not present at the *chokus* in the village, and why people gossiped so much about her.

Before 1958, it was common in Bhutan to abduct people from India as slaves. Because of the high mountains and the dense malaria infested forests on the border between Bhutan and India, these slaves had little chance to escape back to India. The journey from the border of India to Paro or the capital Timphu took five days on foot, through mountains and forests with wild animals. There is a whole village in Punakha were the descendants of the slaves live now. In 1958, after the abolishment of slavery, the King of Bhutan gave all the slaves land. But they are still stigmatised today.

I found out later that society in Bhutan is roughly divided in two strata, "big bones" and "small bones" as the Bhutanese call it. "Big bones" are the nobility and former land owners and "small bones" are the workers or landless farmers. This goes back to the Tibetan division of *sha* and r*us*, *sha* meaning flesh and r*us* meaning bones. "Big bones" are *rus*, the flesh, the nobility, and "small bones" are *sha,* the bones, the landless. The same division exists between men and women. Of course men are *rus,* and women are *sha*, flesh, inferior and also unclean because of menstruation.

Thinley stayed a few days longer and then he told us, "I have to go home, I have to help my parents in the field." We knew he had lost interest but we asked him to make sure that another translator would be sent. He promised. So we had to wait again.

After a week or so a new young handsome guy showed up at my door.

"Hello I am Karma", he said, "and I am your new translator." "Welcome! Please come in!"

Karma was around 18. He looked around and asked: "Do I have to live here?"

"Yes", I said, "this is the way I live."

"I thought you guys would live in tents."

He looked around a bit more, then said, "They wrongly informed me in Thimphu. I thought you were a research team that lived in tents to do the research. This is no fun, I don't want to live with these people."

"What do you mean by 'these people'?" I asked him.

"I'm from an important family in Thimphu", he said, "I am not willing to adjust to this environment."

'What an arrogant guy,' I thought. So I told him it would be better if he left, because he obviously wouldn't be willing to translate or talk to the local people. On the other hand, it was a perfect illustration of the big bones and small bones society.

He left. I felt frustrated. Until now my research was mostly based on observations, and I was so eager to talk to people! And now, again, it wasn't going to happen. The only option now was to go to Thimphu soon and look for a translator myself. Good translators must exist! I learned that living with Aum Zam was a problem for the translators, they were afraid of her. Again the fact that she was a *ngejum* and from the

Zap caste gave her negative power, according to many people.

Our life went on, and I observed all the activities in the village. Little by little, the village had become my world. Thinley had told the *chiepen* (the village messenger) to call me if there was a village meeting, because these kinds of meetings are very interesting.

One day in the middle of the night Pangeh called out to me: "Rieki! Meeting." I thought what? At this time? In the middle of the night?

It turned out that this time was an auspicious time to have the meeting, according to the astrologer. So I put my clothes on and went to the meeting. As far as I can tell, I found out that it was about choosing a new *chiepen*, a position that rotates every year. A messenger has to go to the *dzong* in Punakha to hear what the government of Bhutan has decided in regards to new rules and laws. He also goes to the post office to collect mail. For Marleen and me, the *chiepen* was very important because he brought us our mail.

I learned that nobody was keen on becoming a *chiepen* or a *gup* because it was a lot of extra work. Everybody tried to find ways not to be chosen, but in the end there was always somebody who agreed to do it. Villagers often offered some food or even a small amount of money (if they had it).

CHAPTER 5

SEX IN THE VILLAGE

A t first I was very confused by people's names. Men had the same names as women and there were no family names as we know them in the West. Only the royal family has a surname, Wangchuck, and one other family related to the royals, the Dorji family. Everybody else has a name with a religious meaning, or they are named after the day they were born, like Monday or Friday. Usually a lama gives a baby its name and the result of this is that a whole village can have the same name, because they all went to the same lama and the lama gave all these babies his favourite name.

Close to Punakha there is a temple called *Chimmi Lhakang*, this temple was built by one of the very famous "naughty" Saints of Bhutan from the fifteenth century, Drukpa Kinley. Drukpa Kinley had a holy penis and with this penis he could subdue evil spirits.

He also liked women a lot. In fact, he was known as the divine yogi of crazy sex. He introduced the phallic symbols used in Bhutan, painted on houses everywhere and carved out as doorknobs and in other forms. Drukpa Kinley is one of the most important Bhutanese saints.

For Marleen and me it was very strange to see these images everywhere, they looked pornographic to us. We didn't know the history of the penis images at the time, but it was already clear that the Tsachaphu community was not very prudish. The women were very open about sex and talked about it the whole day, making jokes and gossiping about the size of the private parts of fellow villagers, male and female.

I realised that there was something special about the village women. Apart from their names and their free attitude towards sex, I also noticed the attitude of the men towards them. The men cooked, sewed, took care of babies and mostly were very respectful towards women. It started with Namgeh, Marleen's host. His "wife" was sacred to him. "If Namgeh Bida doesn't like me anymore I have to go back to live with my mother," he told us. "I really don't want to."

"How do you arrange a divorce?" I asked him. "Usually we just separate. Most of the time the man lives with the family of the wife, so when there's a divorce, the man has to go back to his family."

Wow, this is very unusual for a South Asian country, I thought. I asked, "what happens when there is a conflict?"

"Then the couple has to go to the *gup*, he will help them to try to find a solution. Usually this is not needed."

I noticed that Aum Zam was a strong woman who controlled her three sons with an iron fist. I also noticed that at the house of the three sisters the oldest sister was the boss. The three sisters had a big household, all three of them had a husband, and more male relatives were living with them. They were rich because they had lots of land and lots of people who could work the land.

In Tsachaphu there was a severe shortage of labour. This was first time that I lived in a community where money did not play a role; food and labour did.

The household of the three sisters was so rich, they even had their own house monk who took care of the house altar and did all the religious rituals. I noticed that all the men told me, if there was an important decision to be made, normally a family would first consult the astrologer then they would ask the oldest woman in the house. It was the voice of the oldest woman that would be the strongest one, even stronger than the astrologer's voice.

At the beginning of our stay, Marleen lived in Phurba's house. Phurba had a very pretty wife and two adorable children. Phurba's brother was also living with them when he was not in the forest with the cows, and he was sometimes away for weeks in the forest.

During Thinley's brief tenure as our translator, Phurba left for Nepal. He told me via Thinley that he had had enough of Tsachaphu, that people didn't treat him right and since he and his brother were both "married" to his wife, his brother could take care of her. He wanted a break.

I thought this is interesting, a woman married to two brothers? We all knew that the king of Bhutan was married to four sisters, but we didn't know that a woman could do this too. Later I learned this is a

Tibetan custom. Both men and women can marry several spouses at the same time.

In general there was a lot of sexual freedom in the village, for men and women. One of the more unfortunate results of this, however, was that a lot of people suffered from sexually transmitted diseases. One young woman, my neighbour Kinley, had been sick from the moment I met her at the beginning of my stay.

Once a month a mobile health clinic would come and set up a big tent in the forest. They walked all the way up to Tsachaphu with horses carrying the equipment needed to treat people for minor issues for free. From all over the valley people would come to seek out the health workers, one Bhutanese GP and three nurses.

Pregnant women and babies could get a check-up, babies got treatment, and any villager who was sick could get treatment. I spoke to the doctor and he told me that it was very difficult to explain to the villagers how to use western medicine. In general people believed when they got sick they had disturbed a deity or a god. To offset this they thought they had to consult a *ngejum* or a *pow* for spiritual healing. The concept of taking a pill three times a day was very difficult to explain. This was a big problem with antibiotics. Because when people took antibiotics, they felt better after a few days and then they stopped taking the medicine. Since they didn't finish the course of antibiotics, many became resistant to the drug and the infection would get worse. Unfortunately, a lot of people were suffering from syphilis and gonorrhoea.

Kinley, my neighbour, was around 25, married with a baby. When I had a translator, her family asked me all the time to give her medicine. I told the family that I wasn't a doctor but that Kinley needed to go to a hospital. I had heard that there was a small basic health unit in Punakha. It was clear that she couldn't wait much longer.

The family decided to arrange the 12 hour trip to Punakha, and I decided to walk with them.

Kinley's family was wealthy. They had many horses, and I was very surprised that they didn't use a horse for Kinley to sit on. Three strong men from the village took turns to carry her on their back. A wooden stool was tied to their back and Kinley would sit on the stool like a baby on her mother's back. I asked the translator why she wasn't riding a horse.

Was is because it wasn't good for her karma?

"Yes, because the horse has to suffer if she is sitting on it."

"But what about the men who have to carry her?"

"Oh that is a different story." Then I realised you don't see many Bhutanese riding a horse.

A whole procession of villagers all joined us on the walk to Punakha. I wanted to go to the *dzong* to see if there was mail and do some shopping. After 14 days Kinley came back with her husband and she was cured. I understood she had syphilis.

One day a young girl was standing at my door. She told me her name was Demma and she must have been around 14. Later I found out she was an orphan from east Bhutan and was now living with a family in Tshachapu. Because there was no orphanage in Bhutan, young orphans were taken in by families or sent to convents or monasteries, often under very harsh conditions. It always broke my heart to see a young boy no older than six living in a monastery with no motherly care, his head covered in wounds because of the rough shaving of the head and his back covered in whip marks. A similar fate awaited girls in convents who were forced into a religious life they didn't want.

Demma was now 'adopted' by a village family but she was more a servant than an adopted child. Demma was a pretty, skinny girl and very bright. Marleen and I liked her a lot and she had an amazing gift of teaching us Dzongkha. She pointed to things and told us the names in Dzongkha, we repeated them and learned more and more every day. It was a simple process, but it proved quite effective, particularly when a translator had deserted us again.

Demma loved looking at our things and she asked about our clothes. She asked why we had small pants under our clothes.

"What do you mean?" I asked her. She looked at my clothes and showed me my underwear. She said she would like to have a pair of small pants like that. Then I realised that women did not wear underwear in the village. We promised Demma that when we went to Thimphu for our break we would buy her some underwear.

After that I was paying much more attention to the

women because I was wondering how they managed their menstruation. I realised that even the toilet paper I used in the forest created unpleasant rubbish. The sanitary napkins were even worse. Marleen and I decided to collect them and then burn them in a place where no one could see them.

So I was wondering what the village women did. One day I was sitting in the grass near a small stream and a lady from the village came and walked into the water, standing in such a way that the stream was flowing between her legs. She pulled up her kira a bit and I could see that blood was flowing out of her into the stream. But there was no blood on her dress.

"Oh that is how they do it!!" I was amazed that they could control their menstrual flow. I tried to practice this too. It seemed that the village women could control the muscles of their private parts so that their menstrual blood would not flow out.

CHAPTER 6

A SHAMAN RITUAL

had learned in anthropology that in most cultures
the shaman is always a man, but in Tsachaphu
there were several *ngejums*, female shamans, just
like Aum Zam. I had read later that this tradition is
unique in the Himalayas. In Tibet it used to be in the

same as in Bhutan many centuries ago. Women had powerful positions in the communities as shamans, but with the rise of the Gelugpa sect of Buddhism of which the Dalai Lama is the head, all female shamanism was abolished and persecuted.

But in the remote valleys of Bhutan the tradition could survive for centuries, like the strong position of women in Tsachaphu and many other places in Bhutan. Officially all of Bhutan is Buddhist although in the South many people are Hindu, because they are originally from Nepal. But in the villages in daily life people are what is sometimes called "pre-Buddhist" or Bön, which is really the practice of animism, the belief that there is a spirit or soul in all phenomena of nature.

It is this pre-Buddhist belief that I found and still find so beautiful because it respects all of nature. No living creature is less than any other. This could also help to explain the high level of gender equality in the village. In official Buddhism - just as in Christianity, Islam, Judaism and Hinduism - women have a far lower position or value than men. For example, in Buthan I heard the common Buddhist saying that a woman needs to reincarnate five times as a woman to become a man, and only a man can reach enlightenment! This hierarchy of the genders was reflected in the convents in which women who became nuns had no access to higher studies of Buddhism and were not allowed to meditate. Their position was like being servants to monks or caretakers of the temple. But in the village this was different, as *ngejum* women were respected for their wisdom and ability to communicate with the gods.

One evening Demma came to tell me that a child in the village was ill and her grandmother would go into trance that night to talk with the deity that caused the sickness. The grandmother needed to know which spirit had brought on the illness and what kind of ritual was needed to cure the child. She invited me to see her go into trance.

That evening I witnessed something very special. The grandmother was around 60, she had a hunchback and could not stand or walk straight. Like Aum Zam, she had a huge goitre in her neck. When I arrived in the house, she was already dressed in a *ngejum* white scarf diagonally draped around her body and wearing a crown on her head with five peaks (each presenting a goddess of the east, west, north, south and the ether). She also had a drum in her hand. She started to sing, drumming and turning into circles.

Suddenly she stood up straight. It was as if she had changed into a young woman. Her voice changed and she spoke a different language that only her daughter could understand. It was an ancient Tibetan language.

I could not believe my eyes. Her dancing and talking went on for half an hour and after that she sat down and became the old lady with the hunchback again. Her daughter told us that the session had been successful and that she knew what had caused the child's sickness. They knew what kind of rituals were needed to appease the deity. I talked to the child and according to my book "Where there is no doctor", she had all the symptoms of a rheumatic fever, which is easy to treat with aspirin. But I was no doctor and not allowed to interfere. Later I saw her and it seemed she looked well, but if she had rheumatic fever it could have damaged her heart.

Slowly the months were passing by and the weather became nice and warm. The village was becoming my home. I knew all the people and when I bumped into a group of villagers they often asked me to sing the song "Summertime" that I had sung at Phub Dorji's house. I felt at home and enjoyed the beautiful surroundings. Spring came and with spring nature was waking up. Everything became green and flowers were blooming everywhere! I felt like falling in love.

Daily life in the Bhutanese village reminded me of growing up in a traditional Catholic village in the south of the Netherlands. Official Buddhism with its gigantic temples and over the top iconography, Buddha statues and the many, many saints called rinpoches and lamas seemed to have quite a few similarities with the Catholic Church with its many saints, cardinals and rich churches. Just as in the Catholic Church, daily life in Buddhism was about paying off your bad karma and looking towards the next life.

However, I was a bit disappointed with the level of Buddhist knowledge and wisdom in the village. Most people, even the monks, were not very well educated in their religion. Yet, they knew much more about the animistic belief system and this was far more interesting to me.

With spring coming, the change in nature was so

dramatic that I could understand why people believed in the sacredness of nature. Going into the forest was like stepping into a fairy tale. I could imagine dwarfs and elves living there. The trees had so many colours, from all shades of green to all shades of brown to almost black in all kinds of forms and shapes. The tree branches with spiky plants wound around them like mistletoe. This gave the forest a very mysterious and sacred ambiance. Rocks in many shapes, covered with moss and little flowers, and huge ferns added to the sacred atmosphere. Huge blue butterflies and all kinds of insects like golden beetles flew around.

The villagers had small plots of land that were dedicated to a deity that lived there and no one was allowed to touch that land.

The animals now also became more active. The villagers told us to be careful of monkeys, wild boars, cobras and even bears! Sometimes I could hear the barking deer at night. One farmer's face had been badly damaged by a bear. He was attacked some years ago and was very lucky to have survived.

I had learned from Aum Zam that the villagers would never kill an animal. But they liked to eat meat. I also saw the pigs around the house acting very strangely, they were very horny and very active. Later I saw what their food was. In Tsachaphu there was an abundance of marihuana, it grew everywhere. The farmers collected it and boiled it and fed it to the pigs. This explained a lot about their behaviour!

What was not so funny was the way the villagers killed animals. I remembered the night that I came home drunk and found meat hanging in my room. It was beef. Just before that incident, one of Aum Zam's cows had been sick. Because Aum Zam had no access to medicine for the cow, one of her sons pushed the animal off the mountain and it died a horrible death.

When they wanted to eat pork, the villagers tied a pig to a pole and the poor animal strangled itself slowly to death. I had a huge problem with this, but I didn't have the courage to kill the animal with a knife. The villagers choose this way of killing because it kept them free from the actual act of killing that is bad for your karma. I realised that all religions create a high level of hypocrisy. But at least, I thought, the animals had a good life before they died. They could roam around freely and the pigs were intoxicated by the marihuana diet most of the time.

Now spring was here, people started to work in the fields, ploughing and planting rice seedlings. Also there was talk about starting to clean the irrigation channel, which had its source deep in the forest. Again the astrologer monk was asked to find the most auspicious time. Because the source belonged to the deity of the valley, Katschap, the correct rituals needed to be performed.

Spring was a glorious time and people were preparing to visit the hot springs that Tsachaphu was named after. They were hot baths with sulphuric water, about two hours' walk from Tsachaphu. There were three concrete tubs, four by four metres each and the hot water came in through pipes from the well. Close to the baths there was a wooden shack, were people could spend the night. It was very, very basic.

More and more people passed through Tsachaphu on their way to the hot springs. Sometimes we saw whole families with livestock, like cows, pigs and horses to carry their bedding, tents and cooking tools.

People would camp out at the springs for a whole month.

Marleen, I and the some of the villagers decided to go there for the day. We all could use a good bath, I thought. My skin was black, even in my armpits, my belly was red and full of flea bites. The thought of soaking in a hot bath was very tempting. I had images of a nice spa, maybe I could use my perfume now and my nice deodorant that I brought from home. What sheer luxury. I hadn't used it before because it was a total waste and the sweet smell would attract even more bugs.

So we hiked to the hot springs, filled with great expectations.

When I asked if we needed to wear our swimming suits, the villagers said that, because we were not mothers yet, we had to cover our breasts. Women who had given birth only needed to cover the lower part of your body. Legs were considered very sexy and should be covered. Breast were not considered an erotic zone.

For far away we could see the steam rising between the trees. Oh no! I could not believe my eyes. To get to the baths we had to walk for at least ten metres through all kinds of animal droppings. We were covered with mud mixed with excrement up to our knees, because all the animals from the people who were camping there just roamed around freely. "When we get out of the bath we will be even dirtier than before we got in!" I said to Marleen.

The wooden shack was just as dirty as outside and I could feel the fleas jumping up my legs. Quickly we took off our clothes and walked up to the baths. I felt great to smell the rotten egg-scent of the hot water after months of little washing.

All kinds of people were sitting with us in the tub, some older men, who I understood to be monks, some older women (mothers) with their bare breasts and some young guys. The young guys could speak some English, and they told us that they were at the hot spring for religious purposes. They came to meditate and they would stay for a month. They had brought all their food with them. One of the young men told me that he loved English names and he had changed his name to John Scot. His friend told me his name was Peter. Funny, I thought, to me all the Bhutanese names are exotic, but Western names are very exotic to them.

After a while an older man came towards the baths in a very dirty *gho*. He looked like a cow herd who lived deep in the forest with the cows. He took off his *gho* and stood there in his shorts that used to be white a very long time ago. His body was covered with black spots of dirt and I could see the fleas jumping on his back.

"Oh no!" I said to Marleen, "I hope this guy is not getting into the bath!" Yes! He jumped into the bath and just at the spot where the clean water came into the tub, a whole ring of dirt entered the water with him in the middle. All the people in the tub started to scream at him. They told him to sit at the end of the tub, where the water was flowing out.

With a big smile on his dirty face he moved towards that spot. We needed to soak a bit longer to make sure we were not getting the dirt of the cow man on our bodies. Marleen and I tried to think of a strategy to get back to the shack, while staying as clean as possible, so we could change into our clothes. We couldn't think of any, the mix of excrement and mud around the baths was just too much. "At least our bodies are clean now," I said, "and we can clean our feet afterwards in a stream in the forest."

Just before sunset we reached Dengana, the first hamlet in Tsachaphu and Marleen's home. It was almost dark and walking down towards Neptenkha (the hamlet were I stayed) I had to pass a cornfield. I used my flashlight to see the path. Suddenly I heard a noise in the corn field. I shone my flashlight into the field and saw two eyes staring at me. In a split second I started to run on the path towards Neptenkha. This path was very narrow and full of holes and boulders, but for some reason I had wings, I ran like the wind. A big animal followed me. It was a wild boar, which they can be very dangerous. Thanks to the gods of the valley I was faster than the boar, so I reached home safe and with my heart racing.

After staying a month in the village, the *chiepe*n brought me a letter from the ministry of agriculture telling me that a Dutch development worker had started to live in Punakha. He would work with all the farmers from the villages around Punakha, and Tsachphu was part of the Punakha district. It would be good for us to visit him. From then on, once every three weeks I walked to Punakha to do some shopping and to visit this Dutch development worker. This worker lived in a modern house with a bathroom and he baked bread and cooked other delicacies that I did not have in the village. His name was Martin, and he knew everything about animal husbandry. He told me that the cows in Tsachaphu were all very healthy.

I always enjoyed the long walk down to Punakha, although I always went on a Friday and this was a very inauspicious day to travel, but I took the risk. People warned me of aggressive monkeys that could attack me and of course there were snakes. Someone one told me to carry a cloth, and if a cobra attacks you, throw the cloth at it, so the snake bites into the cloth and most of the poison goes into the cloth, giving you time to run away. I always kept this in mind.

During my stay I only had the one incident; the one with the wild boar. All my other walks were fine and I stayed safe.

CHAPTER 7

A QUEST TO TIMPHU

S pring turned into summer and it got hotter every day. And now the most important village activity for our study was coming up: the cleaning of the irrigation channel. The water that irrigated the rice fields came from deep in the forest and we wanted to observe the entire process. I was also aware that the end of our stay was getting closer. I needed a good translator! Once again, we were reduced to observations and to the few people in the village who spoke a little bit of English.

Three translators had left after a few days. Namgey with his jealous wife wasn't really available to us anymore. The young translators were all from well-to-do families and had studied in India, and now they were not willing to stay in a very traditional village without any comforts. So, one day Marleen and I decided to get a good translator directly from the capital Thimphu and we decided to get one ourselves. We took the long walk to Punakha to take the bus to Thimphu.

We were looking forward to our little "holiday", to showers, a real bed and different food. I must have been in much better physical condition now since the whole hike through the fields only took me eight hours instead of the12 hours I had needed the first time! During our walk we were both wearing aWalkman, and I was listening to salsa music and my all-time favourite, Neil Young. We walked to the rhythm of our music, and I was distracted from the dangers of wild animals crossing our path. We enjoyed the nice weather and beautiful landscape. It was a blissful walk!

Very hungry and sweaty we arrived in Punakha and were looking forward to visiting the Welcome Hotel, a little restaurant-cum-bar as they say in Bhutan. It was the only place you could order a meal and have a drink. *Ema datsi*, the melted cheese with chillies and red rice, the staple food of Bhutan, was the only dish they had. A cloth hung from the front door of the restaurant in the Tibetan style. This cloth had once been white with colourful prints of the 10 lucky signs, but now it was black and shiny from dirt and the many hands that had touched it. The "restaurant" had four tables and a bar that sold Eragon rum, Mountain Peak whiskey and Eagle Beer. Eagle Beer was Indian made, the hard liquor was made by the Bhutanese army (a Bhutanese army welfare project), which was mentioned on the bottles. Marleen and I were very hungry and ordered the *ema datsi* with rice with a beer! It was a luxury to eat at a table and have a beer with the meal. While we were waiting for our food, more people came in. A young girl came to sit at our table and started to chat with us. She wanted to know where we were from, which government department were we working for? This was the first question all Bhutanese asked us: not the country we came from. In those days most foreigners were development workers. Very few tourists visited the country.

The girl's name was Phuntsho and she was in high school in Punakha. She came from East Bhutan and spoke English very well. There was a new high school in Punakha and many students stayed there in the dorms. Most teachers were Indians, interestingly all Christian Indians from Kerala. A little bit later two women came in and I could not believe my eyes, they had permed hair and were wearing make-up. During all my time in Bhutan, I had not seen anyone with a perm hairdo and make-up. Most women had short hair. Long hair was only allowed for women who belonged to the royal family.

"Who are the women with these unusual hairdos?" I asked Phuntsho.

"Oh," she said, "these are very strange women because they sleep with men for money."

"What?"

"Yes," she said, "some guys at school told me this. They told me that some of their older brothers were approached by these women, not from Punakha, from somewhere else, who offered to sleep with them if they would pay for it. I find this strange, why would a woman do that?"

This was very interesting, particularly considering that prostitution didn't officially exist in this country. I found it amazing that women had the freedom to do this. Later, when the country opened up, prostitution and human trafficking became a problem in Bhutan just like in India and Nepal but this was mostly in towns bordering India and some cases with tourists.

In the villages, at the time of my first visit, there was a custom for men and women to get together for something called 'night hunting'. Bhutanese houses didn't have window panes, only wooden shutters. If a man was in love with a woman, he would go to the house of his girlfriend at night and climb into the house through the window. Then he would sneak very quietly into the room and sleep with his girl. The only challenge was that the whole family slept in one room. So it was of vital importance for the lover to find the right person in the darkness... Many funny stories were told about night hunting. Nowadays the houses all have glass windows, so night hunting is dying out.

Marleen and I spent the night with two development workers in Punakha before taking the bus to Thimphu next day. But later in the evening I became violently ill, with vomiting and diarrhoea. I thought I was dying. This was the third time that I had food poisoning. That horrible Welcome Restaurant! I shouldn't have eaten there. I knew it would take three days to recover but it was horrible to travel feeling so miserable. Ironically we had to take a bus called the "vomit comet" because many Bhutanese became very car sick and put their heads outside the window to throw up. I felt like this already without riding the bus, but I could control myself and, to be safe, it was of vital importance that we could sit in the front of the bus. The bus driver was an Indian man from Bihar with oiled hair who looked like a villain in a cheap Bollywood movie. But he was very kind and allowed us to sit in the front next to him. Marleen liked him very much and halfway on our trip to Thimphu she said she had fallen in love with the guy. I had to laugh so much.

"I really need a good night with a guy," Marleen said "it will be another two months before I see my boyfriend!"

"Get real," I said, "this guy is probably a truck driver too, you know about AIDS and how dangerous it is to go with a guy like that! Better control yourself." Afterwards we had a good laugh about it and Marleen waited faithfully for her boyfriend at home. But it was a bit hilarious to see her falling for the bus driver.

We arrived in Thimphu and stayed at our concrete

apartment again. But I found I couldn't deal with electric light anymore. It was too aggressive for us now, so we decided to use candles just like in the village.

The next day we went to the ministry of agriculture to talk to our supervisor, a very nice middle aged man who was very kind to us. We explained all the problems with our translators and he understood and promised us to find a very good one. We just needed to wait a few days.

Marleen and I enjoyed our stay in Thimphu, we went shopping, and visited the market. One morning I was walking on the main road and a guy came up to me.

"Are you the *chillip* (foreigner) who is staying in Tshachapu?"

"Yes," I said.

"There was a letter for you but we have send it to the post office in Punakha."

Everyone knew us, it seemed. We continued shopping. We needed to buy underwear for little Demma, and toothpaste for little Tsering, and a few other things for the village.

The gentleman from the ministry of agriculture

kept his word, after two days we received a message that two translators had been found, whom we had to interview. So we went to the ministry to meet the two guys. The young men were about 20 and had just finished their college education in India. They called themselves Max and Peter, their Bhutanese names were Dorji and Norbu. We told them about the conditions and that it was not easy to stay in the village, but these guys didn't mind. They had the right mind-set. Max especially told us that he loved nature and wanted to learn more about traditional Bhutanese life.

Happy and full of good energy the four of us went back to Tsachaphu together. Marleen was happy that this time the bus driver was a Bhutanese monk. We hiked up to the village together and Max loved the hike.

This time Max stayed with me and Peter stayed with Marleen. This way we could go through all our observations and check with the villagers if they had been correct, and if we had understood what we had seen.

For example, I was still intrigued by the male carpenter who was dressed like a woman the whole day at the roof raising party at the house of the three sisters. What did it mean? Was it an ancient custom? My new translator explained it to me. The reason was that the number of women at the party was not auspicious, they needed one more woman, or they would have had to send one woman away, which was very impolite. So one of the carpenters volunteered to be a woman for the day, the number of men and woman was rectified and this way they could fool the gods.

Max turned out to be a real gem, he was very bright and loved being in the village. He basically saved my research and also it was nice to learn how much we had understood just by observing. Maybe people had also trusted us more willingly because we didn't ask them annoying questions. So in the end, maybe it was a blessing in disguise not to have translators all the time. Max would later get a scholarship for Yale in the US, he became chamberlain to the king of Bhutan and the head of a prestigious international organisation.

When the day arrived to clear the irrigation channel, we all prepared to go into the jungle. I had some doubts as to how important this channel really was. It rained a lot in Tsachaphu, and there was a lot of water anyway. But it turned out I was very wrong. We did of course observe the auspicious day and time, but in addition, an important ritual was needed to appease Katchap, the powerful deity of the valley. Marleen, the two translators and I were invited to attend the ritual. We all walked into the jungle, the villagers had food and *arra* with them and the village monk had all his paraphernalia for the ritual. The water source was deep inside the jungle and to get there was not easy. We had to climb over fallen trees, boulders and jungle plants. I had leeches in my shoes and on my legs. I carried some tobacco to put on them, this was the easiest way to get rid of them. Deep inside the jungle, the leeches came from everywhere, even from above, from the trees. We had to be careful not to drink them by accident because they fell into our tea!

Finally we reached the source of the irrigation water. We had to fight our way through the plants to get to a clearing deep in the forest where the spring originated, next to a huge boulder. The boulder was the altar and the villagers put butter lamps and *thankhas* (religious paintings) on the trees. Big baskets with rice, *dzip* and *dzau* (puffer rice eaten as a snack), butter, and *arra* were placed on top of the boulder. In the old days, animals were sacrificed on the altar. But since the 1960s this was not allowed anymore, so people now sacrificed rice, *arra* and other food. Everyone bowed towards the altar and some songs and dances were performed. The songs were generally very old (some dating back to the fifteenth century) and very beautiful. After the ritual, the villagers started to work on cleaning the irrigation channel. A small man, whom I had never seen in the village before, was working very hard. He looked like a mentally impaired person to me. When I asked who he was, the villagers told me the he had murdered his mother. What? But his mother was a bad person, they said, so nobody reported this to the officials. What? I could not believe my ears.

In general I noticed that Tshachapu was a kind of anarchic community. One story told in the village was that the King could never visit this place because the mountain god Katchap would throw stones at him and kill him. I don't know if this was true, but what I know is that the villagers were not happy if a civil servant or government official came to visit. Usually they demanded VIP treatment, the best food and *arra*, and they would not pay for it. Sometimes they even demanded a beautiful girl to sleep with them. So the village people really didn't like too much interference with their lives from outside their community.

In those days it was actually possible for a village to live more or less according to its own rules, up to a certain point. They had a lot of freedom then, but with modernisation and a money based economy coming in, the village way of life changed considerably. After 1990, the year of my stay in the village, even the remotest corners of the kingdom would be 'blessed' with education. The fourth king of Bhutan, a truly benevolent ruler, brought schools to the most remote villages in the land. But I sometimes question if school education is truly a blessing.

When I was in the village, the fact that I could read and write made me special and therefore I didn't need to work in the fields. All the people in the village who were educated didn't have to do the heavy agricultural work. I found out that working on the land was not regarded as "clean" work and therefore bad for your karma. Ploughing the land (a man's job) killed a lot of bugs in the soil. This was bad for the man who killed them. Women had to carry dung in big baskets on their backs and spread the dung on the land. Working with dung was also regarded as unclean.

But if you looked at the custom, free from the religious value judgements attached to it, it was very beautiful. The man penetrates mother earth to put the seeds in her and the women nurtures this with the dung, just like the way humans and other mammals produce babies. This was what I loved in the village society, to learn about the old shamanic ways and to witness their beauty.

CHAPTER 8

NATURE, STATE AND CHURCH

The laws of nature were the highest laws, and people lived their lives observing those laws of nature, much more so than the laws and rules of Buddhism or the state or even the king. I felt very blessed to be able to witness this to its fullest. I never would experience a society with this level of honesty and purity again.

At first, in the beginning of my stay in the village, I experienced every day as the same because there was no "weekend", breakfast, lunch and dinner were the same and people w the same clothes day in day out. Also it was difficult to tell people apart because many had the same name and to me many people looked alike. But I was very wrong!

First of all I learned from the villagers how they lived in close harmony with nature and respected it, the change of seasons, the times for spiritual rituals, the times to work the fields, clean the canals, and many other activities. In our modern lives we aren't so aware of this anymore, particularly those of us who live in big cities. Going to the office every day is disconnected from the change of seasons. In a way, our life is actually the same all year round! If you compare traditional village life with modern money-based life, it's quite remarkable how little time people spend working for their food and shelter. In the modern world, people work 40 hours a week all year. Here, nature provided everything and people only had to work for three to four months to have enough rice for the whole year. Everything else was foraged in the forest or grown in the home garden. Of course it was hard physical work, but not 40 hours a week all year round.

One morning on a gorgeous day in May, it was warm and the birds were singing, I looked out of my window and I at the end of the village where the path towards Punakha starts, I could see a white tent on bamboo poles. "What can this be?" I said to Marleen who had come to visit me.

"Let's check it out", she said.

We walked towards the structure and to our shock we saw two human feet sticking out of the white canvas structure. Underneath, we saw a dead body resting in a foetal position.

"What is this?" we both screamed.

Soon Phub Dorji came to towards us and explained that the dead person was a very old lama who had been staying at a neighbour's house and meditated most of the time, so we never saw him.

"They will take him to Punakha to BBQ him". Phub Dorji said. Of course he meant to cremate him. For us it was an opportunity to learn how complicated and elaborate dying is in the Tibetan Buddhist world. I already knew that all the villagers had only one insurance (paying for it with money or in-kind), and that was a funeral insurance. I saw them paying the village headman for it when there was village meeting.

So why was this dead body lying outside? They even had a guard at night to keep the wild animals away. In Tsachaphu, when someone dies, it is important that the relatives know what star sign the person is, or which animal sign, according to the Chinese zodiac which is followed in Bhutan. After the person has passed away, it is important that the body be placed in the foetal position, which is the way they will be cremated. The person who helps the dead body to get into this position has to be born in a year that is equally strong as the year in which the dead person was born. For example, someone born in the year of the rat cannot be 'handled' by someone born in the year of the snake. Because the snake eats the rat, and so on. If there is no one matching the dead person than someone will be chosen at random and this person's face will be painted black, so the *dzip* or harmful spirit that can be in the dead body can not recognise the person and therefore cannot harm him or her.

After the body is placed in the foetal position, the astrologer decides on the most auspicious moment to bring it outside. This is has been the tradition since Buddhism was brought to Bhutan by Guru Rinpoche, who was an incarnation of the Buddha himself. His teachings direct many aspects of Bhutanese life. The astrologer even has to advise on the best way the dead body can leave the house, through the door, through the window or even through the roof. If necessary, the roof of the house will be opened up for this. When the body is outside, the astrologer will determine an auspicious day and time for the cremation. Most villagers will be cremated at the cremation ground next to the Punakha *dzong*. So the body needs to be carried there. But in the meantime, monks and lamas are invited into the house to perform the *bardo*, the death rituals that guide the dead person to their new incarnation. This is very important and these prayers take 49 days, the time it takes for the departed soul to transition.

At our neighbour's house many people came

to visit, big fires were lit and huge pots were filled with rice and t*sum* to feed everybody. Overall the atmosphere was quite jolly. It was not the custom to cry or to show grief because this keeps the spirit from entering the new incarnation.

I learned overall that death was part of daily life and people talked about it without showing much emotion, at least not like we do in the West. I found out that many families in Tsachaphu had lost a lot of babies. So many children died under the age of three due to lack of hygiene, mostly from diarrhoea. The parents only gave a child a name after it was four years old, when the chance of survival was higher. I noticed that the older children were very strong but some had blondish hair, a sigh of protein deficiency, and all the kids had chronic colds due to lack of vitamin C.

One older couple next door had had nine children and all of them died.

Now they had no one to care for them when they were old and could not work the land anymore. I learned how vulnerable you are if you have to grow your own food. In Tsachaphu there were no shops. The best you could do would be to barter, like dried chillies for cheese or one day's work for a certain amount of rice.

In June the rains started and could last for days. Everything was damp, and I had small lesions on my feet that didn't want to heal. The biggest problem were the flies! I had a million flies in my room, and for the first time I slept under my mosquito net. If I wanted to use my little table for writing up my notes, I had to clean it with kerosene first to get rid of the flies. It was not possible to eat without eating a few flies along with the rice and chillies. The result was that I developed chronic amoebic dysentery. Because there were no latrines in the village and people defecated close to their homes, the flies were feasting on human droppings and those same flies then sat on the food we ate.

In addition to the constant rain, the flies, mud streams and open wounds that didn't want to heal, the rainy season also made it very difficult to find vegetables in the forest. The menu now was mainly rice and butter tea, no vegetables and very little cheese. Before the rains started, people had collected so many delicious things from the forest, such as fresh cinnamon bark that the kids eat liked to eat like candy. Sometimes Aum Zam's son went into the forest to look for *nakhe*, delicious young ferns that taste like green asparagus. I realised again how important it was to be able to work the land. Marleen and I were useless, we couldn't even carry a basket of dung! These baskets were so heavy, but this was actually woman's work. The women in Tsachaphu were strong.

I was really curious about the old couple without children. It seemed they had enough to eat, but where did they get their rice from? They had a home garden where they grew vegetables and the old man went to the forest to collect mushrooms and other things. Later I found out that Phub Dorji would 'lend' the old couple rice, every year. I thought: this is interesting, this couple can never repay him for that rice. Then I learned that in general, poor people are regarded as very powerful because they have a lot of negative power (like the evil eye), which they can use to harm you. The more affluent people are, the more they are afraid of the evil eye. So they do everything to protect themselves, a bit like getting good karma. Phub Dorji gave the poor couple rice. He didn't expect anything in return, and this was good. It kept the balance in a small society like Tsachaphu. Not everyone in the village was cremated. Dead babies were thrown into the river. This was maybe the reason why the villagers didn't eat fish. They told me fish were sacred, but they never explained why. Dead children from the age of three to 14 would be placed on a high mountain top, and there they would be fed to the vultures, a sky burial just like in Tibet.

But we didn't only observe death in the village. Marleen and I also were there to celebrate a birth. Phurba was in Nepal when his wife was due and his brother took care of her. He helped her with the delivery of a healthy daughter. Marleen and I had the feeling that he was the father. He was so proud and so happy to have a daughter. In Bhutan people generally prefer daughters above sons, in sharp contrast to Nepal and India, where daughters are seen as burdens. We had to wait three days before we could visit the mother because it is believed that a woman who just gave birth has a lot of *kaydrip* (defilement by birth), a kind of negative energy and needs to stay in bed with no visitors during that time. Then, a purification ritual (*lhabsang*)

is performed in the house, after which outsiders can
visit to see the new born baby. The child is also taken
to the temple of the local deity and the name associated
with the deity is given. In some cases, the child is given
the name of the day on which the child is born. The
horoscope of the baby known as *kye tsi* is written based
on Bhutanese calendar. It details the time and date of
the birth, predicts the future of the child, rituals to
be executed at different stages as a remedy to possible
illness, problems and misfortune. But in 1990, most
of the Bhutanese had no clue when they were born.
The parents had not registered the children. That is
why most Bhutanese over 35 have 1 January as their
birth dates in their passports (if they have a passport,
of course, which is quite rare).

As I have said before, most families in Tsachaphu
only named their children after a few years, when
they could be more confident that they would survive.
Much later, in a Thimphu hospital, I had a talk with
the first female doctor in Bhutan. This lady was from
Kalimpong in India and was married to the first
doctor in Bhutan. She told me that she used to walk
to remote villages to help women give birth. She also

told me that the villagers have a strange custom. The man who helps the woman with giving birth puts a ball of wool into the anus of the woman, to make sure that the child will come out the right way and not though the wrong hole. I felt sorry for these women, giving birth is already painful enough.

CHAPTER 9

LEAVING THE VILLAGE AND A PIECE OF MY HEART

Now the irrigation channel was cleaned, people in the village had another obligation they didn't like very much. This was *chapdaula* or the traditional tax system. All households had to pay taxes, and in the village that meant providing free labour. At least one member of a household had to work for the government for a fixed amount of days per year or pay this service off with money. Now, some of the villagers needed to go to Punakha to work on the *dzong*. They had to help to maintain and renovate it. When they came back, the men started to plough the fields and the rice seedlings were almost ready to be transplanted. I noticed that in winter time, when I came to the village, life was very relaxed and not much was done. People maintained their homes, collected firewood and slept a lot. We went to bed soon after dark and got up soon after dawn, and the days were short. But now in summer, dawn was at 5 AM and people got up and started to prepare the fields, till it was dark again around 7 PM-8 PM. The most important but also most hardworking months of the year started because everyone's food security depended on them. I asked the people in the village if they could ever remember a famine, but nobody could. I noticed the soil was very fertile. Marleen had brought vegetable seeds with her, and we had planted them: salad, carrots and radish. After a few weeks we could harvest them. But although all houses had home gardens, nobody used them for vegetables. They didn't need to. The forest gave them everything they needed, spices like cinnamon, Szechuan pepper, a variety of spinach, young ferns, many mushrooms and bush tomatoes. But later in the year, the home gardens would be used to grow the most important crop after rice, and that was chillies. A Bhutanese cannot exist without chillies. If there was an increase in price on chillies in Bhutan, this could truly spark a revolution.

I was preparing to leave the village and go back

to Thimphu. But I had a major problem to deal with. Because there was a shortage of labour in the village, all the men were busy working in the fields. There was nobody who could walk with me to Punakha with a horse to carry my luggage. Money payment was of no interest to them, they wanted labour. One neighbour told me if I could work for him in the fields for one day, he would have time to come with me. But I didn't have the skill or the strength to work in his fields. Ploughing with the fierce oxen was too dangerous. I also didn't know how to transplant the seedlings into the mud. Marleen decided to stay a week longer because she needed to finish her technical research. She would take my stuff along with hers when she left, and then the villagers would have more time.

But I had to go back to Thimphu as soon as possible because I had lost too much weight from the constant diarrhoea and I needed to have it checked out properly at the new hospital in the capital. We still had a month in Thimphu to write our reports for the government.

The last night as I was lying in my 'bed' I asked myself what I had learned from my stay here.

I answered: "People are the same everywhere.

Although people in Tsachaphu live a traditional life, they have also jealousy, love, greed, fear and grief. Just the same as everywhere." But the one thing I admired very much in the village was the calmness of the people, the total absence of stress, the contentment and inner peace. What I also noticed was that deep down there is no 'us" and "them". We are all human, with different expressions of culture and belief systems, but even they are all the same at the core. In the beginning the Bhutanese etiquette, dos and don'ts were alien to me, but after a while they made so much sense.

I learned many little things that made life run more smoothly. If you hand something over to someone always use two hands (that is common to most Asian countries, but at that time I didn't know it). If you give something to someone, never give them an even number but an uneven number, never two chocolates but three or five, and so on. Never sit on a pillow that is meant for your head. The human head is sacred, and it should be treated with respect, not defiled by feet or someone's rear end. The same applies to books or pictures of holy people or images of the Buddha.

Feet or the shadow of feet should never touch food or sacred objects or be pointed at people or sacred objects.

After many mistakes I got used to these dos and don'ts and they made sense. I liked the respect that comes from observing them. Later I learned much more about Bhutanese etiquette, many things that are quite comprehensive and exotic.

Shortly after I left the village, I heard someone mention that the fourth King of Bhutan had said that development for Bhutan was needed, but that it had to be done on a conscientious way. It was more important to preserve the gross national happiness than to increase the gross national product. I think I knew exactly what he meant, and he was right. Sadly enough, the whole Gross National Happiness philosophy later became an empty commercial slogan to sell Bhutan. The local people call it Gross National Hypocrites, because the people who run it have no idea what they are doing. In fact, they are an example of gross national unhappiness.

In our last month in Thimphu we needed to write our proposals for the government. We were all back from our villages and exchanged stories about our hardships in the field. Dirk was clearly trying to become a local. He had become a Buddhist and was only wearing *ghos*. We all talked a lot about our experiences. It was obvious that Marleen and I had been in the most difficult location. I lost so much weight and my chronic diarrhoea was not getting better. So one morning I went to the newly constructed hospital, still very small at the time. I had put some of my faeces in a container, so it could be examined at in the lab. Arriving at the counter of the hospital, I met a few farmers with the same problem, only they had put their stool sample in a cardboard box! The stuff was all over their clothes and hands.

The doctor told me I had amoebic dysentery. She was an Indian doctor and she started to scream at me that we Westerners were so weak and couldn't handle any diseases. In other words she was saying, "why don't you go home to your country!" I didn't think that was very nice. Later I heard that there was an Italian doctor doing research in the capital, so I decided to see him. He was much kinder and helpful, and he told me not to eat in restaurants, cook all my food myself and disinfect everything I touched and ate. That was good advice and he also gave me the antibiotics I needed.

Ian and Dirk stayed in the east of Bhutan, and they told us about the massive drinking habits of the Eastern people. Ian and Dirk said that the people in Eastern Bhutan drank all day and used a large part of their produce to make alcohol. Even children were often very drunk. Bhutan does have a serious problem with alcoholism, many men and women suffer from it.

Anita and Rolf stayed in the south of Bhutan in a Nepalese village. In the south, there are a lot of descendants of Nepalese settlers, the *Lhotsampa*, who suffer serious discrimination because they are Hindus. Some Bhutanese justify this by saying that, as Hindus, they can have more wives and therefore are in danger of outnumbering the Buddhist Bhutanese, as happened in Sikkim in the 1970s.

Anita and Rolf told us that their stay was very pleasant. They had a nice clean house to live in and overall their circumstances were much more comfortable than mine. We heard rumours that there was a new law in Bhutan that forbade the *Lhotsampa* to talk in their own language in schools and other state institutions. The law also required them to dress in the uniform Bhutanese style (but in a climate that was much too warm for it) and become Bhutanese like the *Drukpa*. The *Drukpa* are the dominant group, and they are all Buddhists. Later we heard that over 100,000 *Lhotshampa* had been forced out of Bhutan, accused by the government of being illegal aliens although many of these families had lived in Bhutan for generations. However, they were suddenly asked to provide papers to prove it, which was impossible. Anita and Rolf were very concerned about the people in their village because they were all *Lhotsampa* and Anita and Rolf had already seen how their rights were taken away from them.

I could understand the fear Bhutan had, because it is the last independent Himalayan kingdom. Tibet is occupied by China, Sikkim by India and Nepal is in a very bad shape due to the Maoist movement, and the subsequent troubles with the crown prince who murdered most of his family and the bad leadership in general. It seems that Bhutan has managed to hide this dark time in its history by promoting the gross national happiness brand that seems to impress the developed world so much, especially in the West. None of these nations have any clue about what is really going on in Bhutan, but Bhutan has sold itself skilfully to the outside world as the last Himalaya spiritual paradise, Shangri La. The reality is very different. What we already noticed in Thimphu in 1990 was power abuse by the royals, alcoholism, the awful situation in the monasteries, especially when it comes to the young children who are kept there because they have no alternative, and drug abuse issues experienced by young people in the capital.

I was glad that the Italian doctor had advised me to be extremely careful with my food and drink. During my last week in Thimphu, there was an outbreak of typhoid, and we had to disinfect everything. In the meantime we worked on our presentation and in the end we presented it to the minister of agriculture and other members of the ministry. Our presentation was an important event, in an official great hall of the ministry of agriculture. The minister of agriculture was there, he was dressed in a beautiful *gho* with an official scarf draped diagonally over his body and a sword hanging from his hip. The director of the Dutch development organisation was also present but he was "only" dressed in a Western style suit. Many civil servants of the ministry joined too. Our three teams presented the results of the research from the three villages we had lived in. We girls were dressed in full *kiras* and the boys in *ghos*.

Interestingly all three teams came to the same conclusion and gave the same advice, for Bhutan's rice cultivation to stay organic. Because the knowledge the farmers had was so unique and the quality of the rice so high, it would be very valuable to preserve both the knowledge and the quality. We had also found that the farmers in all three villages never had a drought or any other misfortune, so they could always feed themselves. Because the three villages were so remote, it would not make any sense introduce the so-called "miracle seeds" that needed pesticides and fertilisers to grow them. There was no infrastructure, and it would take years to develop it, with questionable results.

The ministry was extremely happy with our research and conclusions. We advised the government to listen to the farmers and promote organic farming just as the farmers had done for centuries.

CHAPTER 10

RETURNS

W hen I was back in the Netherlands, I had a hard time re-adjusting to the Western life style. I missed the people from the village. Sadly, the relationship with my boyfriend from the beginning of my stay in Bhutan did not last long. Short after I returned, we broke up.

I had some Japanese friends in Amsterdam and one friend had a restaurant. I spent much time with my Japanese friend. He introduced me to my husband, who was a customer in his restaurant. A year later I finished my studies in cultural anthropology and received my Master's degree. Shortly after this I got married and supported my husband, who was a magazine publisher, in his business. Life went on, I had a baby boy and worked in my husband's company. When my son was four years old, my husband asked me what I would like to do, now that our son was growing up and didn't not need me any more full time.

In all that time, my love for Bhutan had been smouldering within. A little piece of me was still in the village, listening to the birds, cooking on the adobe stove, celebrating at a ritual.

So I told my husband that what I wanted most was to work in and with Bhutan again. Of course I could probably make money as a tourist guide, but my dream was to produce a documentary about the women of Bhutan. As an anthropologist I knew that the position of women in South Asia wasn't all that good. Especially in India, Pakistan and Bangladesh. What I had witnessed in Tsachaphu was truly unique. Just the fact that there were so many female shamans, the sexual freedom women had, the absence of marriage, the position of women as heads of the household. All in all, a documentary could present quite a unique portrait of women in the Himalayas.

Every year in December the Friends of Bhutan organised a dinner in a Tibetan restaurant in the centre of Amsterdam. The food was mainly Chinese with some Tibetan items like *thukpa*. The only dish they had that was also Bhutanese was *mo mo* (dumplings with meat or cheese). *Ema datsi* was not available.

When I went to the dinner that year, there were around 20 people and one of them was a woman who told me she was a film maker. Her name was Babs and she was around 50, with long bright hennaed red hair. She looked a bit eccentric and told me she was a Buddhist. At the time I thought that would be a bonus. I asked her if she was interested in doing a documentary about women in Bhutan.

"Yes!" she told me, "I would love that. I am a follower of Dilgo Kyentse Rinpoche, just like Richard Gere. Rinpoche lives in Bhutan, he fled Tibet when the Chinese took over. I am very close with his daughter and his wife, who is a nun."

At that time I didn't know who Dilgo Kyentse Rinpoche was, but later I learned he was just as famous as the Dalai Lama and after he passed away, I visited his monastery many times. I have also met his daughter and his wife, the nun who was a medicine woman in Paro.

"Why don't you come by next week so we can

talk about it," Babs said. "Yes, great," I said, "I will be there."

I was quite excited to go to her house on the day she told me, and I stood in front of her door at the right time, but she didn't open. I rang the bell again, no answer. Strange, I thought. I called her when I got home (no mobile phones yet!) and she told me she had forgotten the appointment. It should have been a warning sign for me, but I thought it was a minor event that could happen to anyone. We made a new appointment and again she didn't show up. I thought, OK, let's forget all of this, but then she came back to me, apologising and promising it wouldn't happen again.

When we finally had our first meeting, Babs told me about the famous film school she had attended in New York, that she once had a relationship with Bob Dylan and another with the president of Haiti. I was impressed but found it strange that, with her fancy past, she lived in a humble house and was not well-to-do. We talked about the organisation of the project and what was needed to get this film off the ground. First, we needed to make a research trip to Bhutan. I knew of a Bhutanese journalist living in Amsterdam, and I thought it might be a good idea to ask her if she would be interested in joining us for this project. We also discussed the budget and it was clear that I would have to do some fundraising. At that time it was still relatively easy to get funding for this kind of project. Still, I had to work at it, and Babs did hardly anything to make it happen. With the help of my husband I contacted all the organisations in his network. Sonam, the Bhutanese journalist who lived in Amsterdam, had the right connections in Bhutan and she made it possible for us to get access and licenses to film in Bhutan. This was a major achievement because filming in Bhutan is very expensive and obtaining the right licences is a nightmare. But Sonam made it happen. She was a young woman who had studied in the Netherlands and married a Dutch man. This was a great project for her.

What I found very strange from day one was that Babs did not ask me any questions about Bhutan, concerning where and how we would travel, and what to expect in general. She told me that she had been to Bhutan but illegally, a very strange story, with a *rinpoche*, to visit Dilgo Kyentse Rinpoche. It was a strange story because there are road checks on all access routes to Bhutan and it's almost impossible to travel there illegally. But anyway, maybe this *rinpoche* had the kind of connections that made it possible. Babs was telling me that she was close to all the famous *rinpoches* of the Tibetan world, she was one of the first followers of Dilgo Khyenste Rinpoche and many others. That she had travelled widely in Tibet and the Himalayas, staying in Buddhist monasteries, so I thought she knew all she needed to know and needed no information from me. She also seemed obsessed with expensive clothes and was always wearing long dresses or sometimes very short dresses, too short for a woman over 55! I just hoped she would not wear these short skirts while traveling in Bhutan.

So one day in May the three of us went to Bhutan. The plan was to make a trip all the way to the east and on the way we would interview women about their lives. We would also visit Tsachaphu, because this was the most important part of the project, at least in my mind.

And so, after eight years, I returned to Bhutan.

I was a mother now (if I went to the hot springs behind the village I would be entitled to uncover my breasts!), I had my MA, I had lived and worked in my home country, and I had raised the money for a research trip to make a documentary about women in Bhutan.

It should have been a joyful journey.

We arrived in Thimphu and stayed in a hotel in the centre of town. Sonam and I tried to arrange a car and driver to travel to the east. I noticed that Babs had only her long designer dresses with her. I asked her if she had any decent walking shoes for the hike to Tsachaphu and she assured me she did.

Babs turned out to be very critical of Bhutan. At night she would visit all kinds of people, she would not tell me where she was going, and she did not invite me or Sonam to join her. The next morning at breakfast she would say to me: "This country is a dictatorship, everywhere you go you see pictures of the king. This is something you only see in communist states and countries with a dictator. Even the director of the Dutch development organisation, who I visited last night, said the same thing."

Oh that's nice, I thought, you visited him without Sonam and me.

"There are roadblocks everywhere, they have total control over where we go," she continued.

"These roadblocks are there for safety, you know how dangerous the roads are in Bhutan," I said. "There is no telephone and no communication, these roadblocks can control the situation if there is an accident or a landslide." On the way from Paro to Thimphu and on all of Bhutan's roads there are roadblocks, and you need a travel permit to be able to travel from one valley to the next. It is true that this is for political reasons, as well as for safety.

"Bhutan is located in a very difficult geographical area," I told Babs, "with the Assamese guerrilla who fight for an independent Assam on Bhutanese territory." Many accidents and incidents had happened because of the Assamese guerrilla, who attacked farmers and buses full of travellers.

"You are naïve," she said.

"You have no idea what you are talking about," I responded.

Not a good start to a collaborative research project in a foreign country.

Later I noticed that she was only interested in the *rinpoches* and members of the royal family.

After a few days we left for Tshachapu, Babs in her long designer dress and elegant shoes.

"Are you planning to go to Tsachaphu like that," I said. "Yes," she answered, "I can change in a restaurant on the road to Tsachaphu."

I had to laugh. I knew there were no restaurants at the roadside, but I didn't want to tell her that, she would find out herself. We drove along, and it was clear there was no restaurant. We arrived at the place the road ended and the hike to Tsachaphu started. Babs needed to change but there was nowhere to change. We had organised a guide and a porter to help us and they were waiting for us in a rice field. The three men were staring at Babs, she looked very exotic and flamboyant with her red henna hair and long green silk dress. There was not much privacy to change, so she only put on her hiking boots and hiked up in her long dress.

It was a hot day and the sun was very strong. For me it was magical, hiking up to the village again after eight years. My memories streamed back, and it felt all very familiar.

My love for Bhutan swelled up inside me. Yes, this was where I wanted to be. It had been far too long.

I saw that Babs' skin got redder with every hour we walked. The sun was very intense. Babs did not say much. I have to admit I was impressed with her stamina.

In the early evening we arrived in Tsachaphu and agreed to stay in the house of the three sisters. They were very happy to see me. It was a joy to eat the delicious farm food again and drinking the butter tea. I remembered how much I had disliked it the first time, but now it had the taste of a long-lost home. Okhum and Nakhum (two of the three sisters) told me that life had become much harder for the women in Tsachaphu because all the children were going to school now. Before, the children would go into the forest with the cattle but now the men had to do that, so all the farm work was now in the hands of the women. When I was in the village in 1990 there was already a labour shortage, but now in 1999 it had become more severe. Okhum also told me that many people on their way to the hot springs wanted to stay at their house, expecting food. Although they would pay for it, the sisters simply didn't have enough food to sell to them. Also on some days, just too many people came by. I felt sad for the sisters that their lives had not improved. My professor once told me, when modernity comes in women loose. And this was the case for the sisters.

I asked about the all the villagers, how everybody was.

The sisters said: "Phub Dorji has leprosy." I could not believe my ears, this handsome kind man who wanted to give me a baby. Aum Zam was still alive and kicking, we planned to visit her the next day. Sonam and I enjoyed being in the village very much. Sonam saw how beautiful and authentic the village was, and she liked the food just like I did. I suppose in a way a part of me became a bit Bhutanese after my first stay in the village. It certainly felt, smelled and tasted like home.

We made our beds in the altar room. We had brought camping gear so we would be comfortable at night and a spray against bugs, going to bed as soon the sun set, exhausted from the long hike.

I felt very emotional to be back in the village. The villagers acted as if I had not been away at all.

I remembered that I had learned this during my first stay. The people in the village live completely in the present. It was bad luck to speak of the past or the future. I could never ask when a certain meeting or a *choku* was going to happen, it was always the time after tomorrow. When we visited people they never greeted us or said good bye. Sometimes I thought I was not welcome and wanted to leave, then my hosts would come and offer me tea and snacks. It was very confusing. Time, as we know it in the West, linear time, did not exist.

Once I offered my translator a cigarette and he declined. He said: "I don't smoke." Half an hour later, he took out a cigarette and lit it.

I asked him: "I thought you didn't smoke?"

He told me: "When you offered a cigarette I didn't smoke, now I do."

Another time, my translator was cooking *tsum*. I asked him, "do you put cheese in the tsum?" The translator said no. Ten minutes later I saw him putting cheese into the curry. Then I had a eureka moment. I started to understand the whole time concept in the village where there were no clocks or calendars and people didn't know how old they were. Only the astrologer decided when it was the right time to do something, not a date on the calendar or a clock time. This also explained why people did not greet you. When you were there you were there, simple as that.

Now back in the village, I felt so welcome and at home. The only change was that three sisters now did have a clock in their house. We woke up in the morning and Nhakum was making breakfast, rice, *tsum,* and butter tea. Babs was not in her bed and Nakhum told us that she had gone outside very early. I thought I hope she does know that there can be cobras outside, you need to know where to go. Usually any place pigs roam around is safe. Sonam and I brushed our teeth, dressed and washed our faces outside with a bucket of water, and sat down for breakfast. From the window we called to Babs. A little later Babs came in, she told us she had been sitting in a rice field to do her mediation. I told her about the snakes and she didn't respond. Nhakum served us rice and *tsum* and Babs started to complain.

"Don't they have bread? I want to eat bread for breakfast and I want coffee."

"Do you see wheat growing here, or coffee beans?" I said. "No," she said.

"So how can people bake bread if there is no wheat and how can they make coffee if there are no coffee beans growing here? I thought you know these countries so well, but now it seems you know nothing! You have to eat what people have and they are generous enough to share with us, even if we pay for it." I was so annoyed with this woman.

"You are romanticising this village," Babs said, "it's not as great as you say it is."

"You don't know anything about it. This is a unique village, very beautiful, look around you. But you are not willing to see the beauty," I said. I became more and more irritated.

After breakfast we visited Aum Zam, it was so nice to see her again and she looked very well. When she saw Babs, she started to laugh and told us that she had seen Babs that morning sitting in the rice field but she thought it was a monkey because of her red hair. For the rest of our stay in the village we talked to the women in Tshachapu, but it was obvious that Babs was not willing to do anything in the village. It was too much hassle for her, and she wanted to stay in comfortable hotels. Not the film maker I thought she would be and this became clearer every day.

I was sad to leave Tsachaphu behind, but of course we were there to do the research for our documentary, so we drove to Mongar in the east of Bhutan.

In Mongar we started talking to ladies who were sitting on a bench in the middle of town. I was always impressed with the older people in Bhutan. They had this amazing energy, always smiling and telling naughty stories. Their eyes sparkled in brown faces full of wrinkles, they were so beautiful they didn't need plastic surgery. We interviewed the women about their lives and they shared their life stories with us.

In Bhutan, a lot of women from the rural areas prepared for their death from the age of about 45. For us that seems very young but life expectancy wasn't very high in Bhutan at the time. One lady, Namgey, was told us her story.

"I live in a *gompa*, a special monastery for older people, I meditate and read the *sutras*, the holy texts. My children all live in Thimphu, in a small apartment. They have full-time jobs and they have no time and space for me. Now I spend my days preparing for my death, but I like it in the *gompa*, I have my friends and everything I need. When I was young, I inherited the farm from my mother but now I cannot work on it anymore and I have leased it to a family from Tashigang, a place in the far east of Bhutan." This is the kind of story we heard from many older people.

Later we walked through the main street of Mongar and heard drum beats. It was the kind of drum beat that tells you that there is a big ritual or *choku* going on. Sonam and I spent some time in a shop and Babs walked ahead with a camera towards the house the sound came from. We didn't think anything about it. When we were finished in the shop we tried to find Babs but we couldn't see her any more. We walked towards the house where the sound of the drums came from, and there she was, in the middle of the living room, filming everyone. Sonam was very upset. She said this is a funeral, these people are having a ritual for a dead relative. You cannot barge in like that and film these people without an invitation.

Babs said, "but they have pictures of the rinpoche on the altar!" Sonam started to cry and said: "this has nothing to do with you, you cannot just intrude here and start filming!"

I was very upset too and also a bit embarrassed. I felt that I couldn't have my name attached to this person. And also, I was the one who had raised the funds for all this!

The trip ended a week later. Babs became more and more unbearable. She was only interested in the royal family. As it happened, Sonam was a close friend of the younger sister of the four queens. She helped Babs to get access to her and in the end Babs made a documentary of the life of this royal lady.

The film was banned in Bhutan.

I stopped working with Babs. To me, she was not at all a Buddhist, as she claimed.

But my love for Bhutan had been re-ignited. I never wanted to stay away again for so many years.

CHAPTER II

HIGH VALUE, LOW VOLUME

I had to find another way to go to Bhutan on a regular base, and I realised that the easiest way was indeed to be a tourist guide. It was a way to get a visa, see the changes that happened in the country and get paid for my work.

In 1999, at first sight not much had changed apart from the introduction of TV to the country, and the internet was coming. The government started to promote sustainable tourism, meaning expensive tourism. To be able to preserve the pristine nature and culture, tourism should be "high value low volume", tourists should pay a high price to be able to visit the country. In the beginning I agreed very much with this policy because it kept the backpackers out and high-end tourism would benefit all Bhutanese because a big proportion of the money coming in would be tax that could be used for infrastructure, education, health and culture – all sorts of good things.

Until 2007 I guided two trips to Bhutan per year. Most of them took 14 days and we travelled all over the country.

My first years as a guide were a sheer joy. I had mostly Dutch people in my groups and my travel agency organised high-end excursions guided by experts in the field. My clients were mostly elderly people who were retired, interested in culture, and had seen most of the world. What I always found very strange was that when I asked them, "why do you want to go to Bhutan?" They would reply, "because it's untouched and not touristy."

"But you are a tourist…"

Tourism is a very strange phenomenon anyway. What I learned from working with my groups was that they expected an authentic, "untouched" country, but at the same time they expected good hotels with Western style hospitality. I learned that if the food and hotel room are not good, there will be a lot of complaints. I also learned, especially with groups that consist of one nationality, that people have a tendency to cling together, as if they are scared of the foreign environment.

But overall, my first ten years of guiding were very nice, the people were very interested and wanted to learn. In the evenings we had discussions about Bhutan and Buddhism. One group was very special to me, this was a group that consisted of psychiatrists and social workers from the Netherlands. They were the most compassionate and interesting people I ever had. One lady, now retired, had worked a lot with former paedophile convicts. She was skinny, dressed in black leather, with very long black hair. She looked like an older version of a rock star. My Bhutanese guides called her Michael Jackson. This lady told me that she was on a quest to find the most ideal country in the world. She had been to North Korea, but that country was far from being ideal. It was not the socialist paradise. "While I was visiting the hospital in Pyongyang," she said, "all the sick people in the beds were wearing makeup."

She told me how hard it was to work with paedophiles since nobody wanted to deal with them. We know that more people than we would like in this world are paedophiles. In Bhutan there are hundreds of male monks from the ages of 6 to 70 plus living together in big monasteries, and there is a lot going on. It's just not healthy to put so many boys and men together without any sexual release. We are all very hypocritical about it. That was why I had the greatest respect for this lady who was so compassionate and non-judgemental. When I asked her what she thought of Bhutan, she told me, "This country is far from being a happy country as they claim it is, too much poverty, too little freedom, they still have a long way to go."

After ten years of happily guiding in India and Bhutan, I noticed that the groups started to change. Now I had a lot of people who thought that because they paid a lot to go to Bhutan, they thought they would stay in five star hotels. During the time I was a guide there were not many 5 star hotels in Bhutan and the ones that did exist were excessively expensive, like $750 per night and up. One hotel group, the Aman Cora, charged $1,500 per night. The tourists who stayed in these hotels were mostly rich Americans. So we stayed in the best hotels run by the Bhutanese. Some were very good family businesses, more like bed and breakfast places. Usually my groups had no problem with staying in those simple hotels. The only problem was that the beds were very hard and the food, specifically cooked for the tourists, was pretty much the same everywhere. I always missed the farm food that I loved so much. If possible I would eat with my Bhutanese drivers and guides. This food was way too spicy for the guests.

Because I had studied Bhutanese Buddhism for more than ten years, I was able to explain a lot to the people. This Tibetan form of Buddhism is very complicated and you have to study it deeply to be able to understand it. The iconography is very rich and complicated, but also very fascinating, of course. However, some of the tourists started to complain, saying I was talking too much or too little, it was never good enough. Most people were more interested in the hotels and the food than in the country. Every morning they were talking about the showers (if they worked or not, if the water was hot or cold), if the bed was too hard, if there was a shower curtain. Many people seemed to be totally obsessed by the absence or presence of shower curtains. I learned that the basic conveniences are very important to people while they are in a strange country. I would have loved to talk more about their impressions of the country, like with my first groups.

I never forgot one incident in my guiding career that was very special. The elite of Bhutan consists mainly of two prominent families. The number one family is the Royal Wangchuk family and family number two is the Dorji family. The mother of the fourth king is from the Dorji family and this family has a problematic past in Bhutan. Original the Dorji family is a noble family from Tibet and Sikkim. The Wangchuk family is from Tongsa in central Bhutan. The Dorji family was powerful in Kalimpong India during the time of the Raj. They were very enterprising and became very wealthy. In the 1960s a member of the Dorji family became prime minister of Bhutan but he was quickly assassinated by a Tibetan mistress of the third king of Bhutan.

One very wealthy and colourful member of the Dorji family was Dasho Rim (*dasho* means "sir" or a person of noble birth and *rim* is short for *rimpoche*, a high incarnated lama). Dasho Rim was well known through all of Bhutan and beyond, he owned hotels, shops, airlines, estates, etc. He was very eccentric and revelled in shocking behaviour but people loved him. One day I arrived in Phuntsholing, the border town between India and Bhutan, at the Druk hotel which belongs to the Dorji family, with my group of 15 tourists. It was early evening and I was in the mood for a very cold beer, so I went to the hotel bar. Two seats away from me, an older Bhutanese man was also having a beer. There was no one else at the bar, only an Indian-looking woman in her 40s, sitting further away at a table, reading. I took a sip of my beer and the Bhutanese gentleman started to talk to me: "Where do you come from?"

"The Netherlands," I said.

"Oh," he said, "the Dutch make great guns."

"I don't know," I said, "because I've never used a gun and I'm not planning to do so."

He smiled and I realised this must be the infamous Dasho Rim. I knew that he was an incarnated high lama and a very wealthy business man, but I could see he was also an alcoholic. Then he said out of the blue: "I'm fucking afraid to die."

"That is strange," I told him, "you are a *rimpoche* and *rimpoches* should know all about death and dying. You are a Buddhist and in Buddhism the reason to live is to die."

"Yes," he said, "but I'm still afraid to die."

"I'm not afraid to die," I said.

He looked at me for a while, then said: "If you're not afraid to die, why don't you kill Sadam Hussein."

"I don't think that would not make much of a difference," I said, "if I killed him, someone else, maybe an even bigger asshole, would take over. Just by killing people you will not change situations."

"Oh", he said, "I see you have no balls in that pussy of yours."

I had to laugh because the barkeeper, an Indian gentleman, was blushing when he looked at me.

"Why don't you come over to my house this evening," Dasho Rim said, "we're going to have a party. I will give you meditation." I knew what this meditation would mean, haha!

Then he pointed to the lady at the table and said: "I need to talk to that woman, she is from the India Tata family and wants to talk business with me, but

I am sick of talking business. The party tonight is especially for her."

Of course I didn't go to the party because I needed to take care of my group, and we had to get up very early the next morning. After our breakfast, the group boarded the bus to go on to Thimphu. It was still very early, and there was Dasho Rim, standing next to our bus.

He came up to me and said: "Where were you? I waited for you all night!"

I told him I had to take care of my group, so I could not come. Kesang my Bhutanese guide walked up to Dasho Rim and asked him for a blessing. What happened next shocked me very much, Dasho put his hand on Kesang's head, Kesang bowed down a bit and Dasho said: "Go to hell".

Funnily enough, the driver and the other guide started to laugh. I didn't think that it was very funny. I asked the guides later why they laughed, they told me that they knew Dasho Rim would do something naughty and that they liked it. They all told me that he was a good person. I noticed that he was loved throughout the country but that he did do a lot of shocking things (like standing on top of a huge landslide and firing his revolver into the air). This is why the people in Bhutan called him the incarnation of the divine madman Drukpa Kinley, the one who started the penis sculpture fashion.

CHAPTER 12

A HOLISTIC SOCIETY

A fter the documentary trip I didn't only start guiding, I also decided to get my PhD, and started to work on my dissertation. I had so many more questions about Bhutan and I wanted to understand my research findings from Tsachaphu in 1990 even better. I realised now that what I had experienced in Tsachaphu was a holistic society in which people lived in the present, truly sustainable, in harmony with nature and with a lot of gender equality. All these concepts were "hot" in the 90s new age movement. It was also a living example of the eco-feminist movement that started with the work of Rachel Carson's "Silent Spring". What I had not anticipated was that there was nobody at the university who could guide me, there was no professor at that time who had knowledge of Bhutan. I had to make do with my philosophy professors who were really amazing. After several happy and some not so happy years I obtained my PhD in 2008. Strangely it did not bring the fulfilment that I thought it would bring. Actually it brought me confusion. I was lost, my work was done. There was an emptiness. I had loved working on my book. Together with my dog I went for long walks in between writing sessions. During those walks I could think about what to create next and let my thoughts go. As I look back on it now, it was a very happy time.

I have a love/hate relationship with the world of academia. I love to study, search for answers to the questions and I enjoy the fact that you can dig in deep.

But academia also has its restrictions, now I want to write my own story freely and creatively.

In 2007 I travelled through Bhutan again as an academic, doing some more research for my PhD. After that year the biggest change the country ever experienced happened. Democracy would be installed the next year and the crown prince would soon take over. The fourth King was the last absolute king. Also for the first time I could use my mobile phone. Many new hotels were constructed, and a few more luxury five star hotels were established in the country. The number of tourists who could visit the country increased from 5000 per year to 20,000. In 2012 it increased to 120,000!

So many changes and not all for the better. I was worried for my beloved country, and at the same time I understood that some of these changes were inevitable. Others, however...

Before entering Thimphu valley there is a site where the biggest Buddha of the world has been built, but it is a Chinese Buddha, paid for by a rich Taiwanese and it seems he paid millions of dollars for it (talking about ego in a Buddhist country!). The beautiful old small town of Wangdi next to the *dzong* has been destroyed and this town has been rebuilt as a satellite town on a paddy field a few kilometres from the *dzong*. A very ugly concrete monster. Box-like houses with no soul nor aesthetics. It is true that the old town of Wangdi was a fire hazard, but it is sad that the town was not renovated but entirely destroyed. This has also happened to the old town of Punakha that I knew so well from my first time in Bhutan when it was our gateway to the big world beyond the village.

Bhutan joined the rest of the world, consumerism increased, more cars were on the road, more shops and ugly Indian style concrete shopping malls and everybody had a mobile phone. It made me a bit melancholic. Bhutan used to be like a refuge from the rest of the world, but now, Bhutan was not so special anymore.

In spring 2009 I went to Bhutan to guide a group of 15 wealthy Dutch people. This group was special group, all the very wealthy seven men were bankers with their wives, and one very rich single woman who travelled a lot. Most of them had houses in several financial centres in the world.

This group booked a 14 day trip up to central Bhutan. One day we were on our way to a convent in Tang, a valley in Bumthang (Bumthang consists of four valleys and Tang is the third valley coming from the west). This convent is a big square building with small rooms facing a patio, beautifully situated on a hill. It belongs to the Nyingmapa school of Buddhism, the oldest school in Tibetan Buddhism. There were around 100 nuns (mostly young girls) in the convent. Some of them were just orphans, they had no choice but to live like nuns. One girl told me she was so homesick, she came from the east of Bhutan and had nowhere to go now her mother had died. She didn't know who her father was. Another girl told me that she wanted to commit suicide because she was in love with another girl at the convent and she said she knew that her love was very bad and unnatural, so she thought the best thing would be to end her life. All heart breaking stories, but a reality in Bhutan. For us Westerners visiting the country, this convent on top of a hill in pristine nature looks so beautiful that you think it is like a place in heaven. But the harsh reality is different.

We were driving up the steep hill and as we came to the top, I could not believe my eyes. This was the last thing I would expect in this place! In front of us stood a huge helicopter! "What is this?" "What is this thing doing here?"

At that time Bhutan didn't have helicopters, this one had to have been leased in India.

I saw that the path to the entrance of the monastery was decorated with ribbons and on the ground were juniper branches instead of a red carpet, a sustainable alternative to a red carpet in the Bhutanese tradition. Juniper branches are considered auspicious and are also used as incense to chase away the evil spirits.

There was a sign above the door saying, 'Welcome National Geography Team'. Khandu, my Bhutanese guide said: "There must be some VIPs here because the Gangte Tulku is here." The Gangte Tulku is the *rinpoche* who started this convent and he plays an important role in emancipating the nuns in Bhutan, to make it possible for them to study higher Buddhism. Before him, nuns had no access to the higher learning, and they were mainly caretakers or servants to the monks.

We approached the building and inside the building was a big courtyard where a Bhutanese tent was erected, a white tent decorated with colourful auspicious signs, and a whole group of important looking people were sitting in a row next to each other. The Gangte Tulku was sitting in the middle on a throne, a skinny middle aged man wearing dark glasses, with a jug with fruit and flowers in front of him.

In front of the VIPs were about 20 Bhutanese girls in colourful *kiras*, dancing traditional dances, and around them were farmers from the neighbouring villages, and nuns sitting in the grass enjoying the spectacle.

One of the ladies in my group asked me if it was alright to go the VIPs and introduce themselves. She had the self-confidence that comes with being rich and privileged. I said: "Of course this is up to you." She and a few other women went to the tent to receive a blessing from Rinpoche.

While the women walked to the VIPs in the tent a gentleman approached me and he looked familiar. He had a glass eye, and I thought to myself that he looks like Robert Thurman. So I asked: "Are you Robert Thurman?"

"Yes," he said.

"It's an honour to meet you," I replied, "did you come on that chopper?"

"Yes!"

"Isn't it a very noisy way of travelling", I asked him.

"Too much disturbance for the nuns and monks who meditate in the caves in Bumthang," he said. I agreed!

Robert invited us for lunch with all the VIPs who turned out to be Michael Dell from Dell computers and his daughter who had received the Bhutan trip in a chopper as her twelfth birthday gift.

In the tent the nuns offered us a very lavish lunch: many different kinds of *ema datshi*, red rice, dried beef in chilli sauce and many more delicious dishes. Through the years and especially during my stay in the village, I learned to love Bhutanese food. Especially Bhutanese food that is cooked in the villages. It has the authentic taste. Not so much the food cooked in the hotels for the tourists, this food is quite bad and tasteless. But most foreigners don't appreciate the spicy

Bhutanese dishes. After lunch we were invited to join them for some photo opportunities and then the VIPs retreated to their chopper. It was so funny to see the helicopter surrounded by dogs, cows and local farmers who were having a picnic next to it. The helicopter was a novelty for the local people and they had come from all the villages around the convent to see what was happening. The dogs and the cows almost got a heart attack when the chopper took off with a lot of noise and dust. They all ran away for their lives.

CHAPTER 13

MY BEAUTIFUL FOUNDATION

My group of bankers and their spouses went back to our bus to return to Jhakar village, and of Jhakar town. "This land belongs to Druk Yul tours and travels," Khandu said, "and they would like to build a hotel on it. They are looking for an investor." Druk Yul was the name of the travel agency I worked with for many years.

It's a stunning piece of land and an ideal location for a five star hotel, I thought. The view from the land was onto forest and mountain tops, and at the bottom of the hill was a mountain stream. You could hear the water from up here and in the distance you could see the Jhakar *dzong*. I thought this would be a cool project, maybe I could help them to create this hotel. Wouldn't this be fantastic? I decided to talk to

157

Ugyen, the CEO of the travel agency, when I was back in Thimphu.

In the meantime back at the hotel in Jhakhar, Bumthang, one of my clients, was throwing a tantrum. He was an investment banker and he needed to check the Dollar-Yen situation, he needed access to a computer and he wanted to have a gin tonic. No tonic in Jakhar and no internet connection available. And to top it all off, the banker was very upset because there was no wardrobe in the room to hang his clothes in.

In his frustration he commented: "This country needs a hotel school!"

I thought: this is brilliant. An eco-hotel and hotel school are needed here. Why don't I do it myself!

A few days later in Thimphu, Ugyen and I were sitting at the dinner table and I suggested to Ugyen that I could help him with setting up the hotel. Through my husband I have access to the financial industry, investors, banks and the sustainability world. And I have a good network in the tourist industry.

"Are you interested to do the hotel as a social entrepreneur," I asked Ugyen, "to set an example by building a completely carbon-free culturally-authentic hotel? A true luxury hotel that will be set up like a Bhutanese nobility house, each room decorated with beautiful Bhutanese textiles and colours. There will be an altar room, just as in the houses of the nobility and there will be a monk on the premises for people who would like to meditate."

I could picture a cuisine of Bhutanese fusion food. Bhutanese food is simple but the ingredients are very good and organic. I could see it right there and then, a totally new concept for hospitality: five star hospitality Bhutanese style. To make this possible we could establish a hotel school for hospitality training and community development on the premises.

There are so many unemployed young people in Bhutan and the hospitality sector is growing, but hardly any well trained hospitality staff are available to work in the hotels. In general the management of the bigger hotels in Bhutan is very bad. Hygiene in particular needs to be improved. Bhutan chose high quality tourism but didn't really invest in improving the sector. The smaller family run guesthouse are better, but there is still a lot of room for improvement. Lack of professionalism will affect the industry in this country. You cannot expect people to go on paying a premium price for bad accommodation and bad food.

"Yes," Ugyen replied: "I like this a lot. The combination of a high-end hotel and a hotel school. This way we can give back to the community."

WHEN I RETURNED HOME, I TALKED TO MY HUSBAND ABOUT MY IDEA.

"I have the contacts in Bhutan," I said, "good and reliable people, I have knowledge of Bhutan – I've been involved with the country in different fields for over 20 years and have been working in the tourist industry for more than 15 years. I know all the hotels and what people want while traveling there."

An added bonus was that my husband is a highly respected thought leader in the impact financial sector, and he has an extensive worldwide network in the world of investment. So I thought, we hold all the right cards here, so why not do it.

My husband agreed. "Go for it," he said.

I learned from my husband not to talk too much about a project you want to do. Too much talk can kill it because everybody will have their own opinion.

Especially people who've never done anything in their lives. They often have the biggest mouths, although they have no clue what they're talking about. So basically I kept this project to myself and started to work.

BUT WHERE TO START?

First, I had to set up a foundation for the non-profit part. And to be able to do that, I needed good people. Especially a good treasurer who knew finance. I thought of Adrian, he was a very nice man who had travelled with me to Sikkim two years ago and who used to be the CFO of a big Dutch multinational company. Now he was retired, and I was over the moon when he agreed to be the treasurer of my foundation.

I also asked Peter, the owner of the travel agency I worked for. And Mrs Oudenhuis, a friend who had travelled with me many times to Bhutan, a wealthy woman who used to be married to a very rich Dutch businessman. I thought it would be good for the image of the foundation to have her on the board. She was in the group of bankers I travelled with when I got the idea for the hotel and hotel school in Bhutan.

I also added a designer and a Bhutanese citizen who lives in the Netherlands. We had several meetings, discussing the website, the brochure and how to proceed. In summer 2009 the foundation was ready. The name of my foundation, "The Learning Exchange Foundation" just came to me in a flash, maybe inspired by my deep feelings for Bhutan. I could feel my love burning brightly as I started working on the project. In many ways, it was the outward manifestation of my love affair.

In April 2010 I went to Bhutan with Wangmo, a Bhutanese board member in my foundation, who was always so helpful. When it was necessary to go to Bhutan and to explore what would be the best way to set up the project, she invited me to stay with her family, this way I could save hotel costs. While in Bhutan it became clear that this project was exactly what the country needed, and we received a lot of goodwill from the people and the government. Together with Ugyen, the CEO of the travel agency, we went to Bumthang to see the land.

Ugyen arranged a meeting with the minister of finance and other important people who were knowledgeable about the FDI (Foreign Direct Investments) regulations and licensing. That year Bhutan was opening up to FDI and the country needed investments to develop the market and to create jobs. Bhutan was facing more and more youth unemployment.

Bhutan has a population of around 700.000 people, more than 50% of which is under the age of 25. Bhutan also has one of the smallest economic markets in the world. There is not much scope for young people to find a job. The two pillars of the Bhutanese market are hydroelectricity and tourism. Tourism is by far the sector that creates the most jobs, after agriculture. But agriculture is still in a traditional state and farmers have difficulties selling their products due to the lack of a good infrastructure in the country. Another major issue is that many young people now have a high school education up to class 12, and their parents, who are often not educated, put tremendous pressure on their children to obtain a good job as a civil servant. Only a happy few have the chance of a government job with all the benefits. The children who graduate from class 12 often have no clue what to do next, how to find a job or to plan their future. They don't receive any guidance. This is a tragic situation that sadly often ends in suicide. Bhutan, my beloved country, is now known for high suicide rates among young people. Other problems are gangs, drugs and alcohol abuse. To create a school that guides these kids and gives them a future was dream of mine.

I realised that our project could really help the country, and we could develop it into a true impact investment project. Impact investment is a new name for sustainable investment, which refers to investing in a project that is green and benefits the community by creating jobs and makes a profit.

My aim was to build the hotel and school in a truly sustainable eco style, to be an example of eco building techniques with traditional elements and modern methods, including the knowledge transfer to the local industry during construction. The hospitality school for the training of young Bhutanese people for the tourist industry should provide training in all fields. Food and beverage, cuisine, housekeeping but also guiding, bird watching and wellness treatments. During the trip it became clear that we were on the right path. This was and is a great project and fits the country, on a small scale with a big, positive impact.

Ugyen, the Bhutanese travel agent, arranged meetings with the secretary of finance, the director of finance and the director of labour. All the bureaucrats assured me that my project was the right thing to do and just what the country needed. Ugyen made it very clear to me that if we want to build a good, sustainable hotel we needed a Western architect, so I told him that I would look for one in Europe.

For a project like this, it is of vital importance to have a good local partner. Ugyen and his two other partners had an excellent reputation in Bhutan. They were respected by all their employees and government bureaucrats at the highest levels. Ugyen was around 50 and a very serious man. He didn't smoke or drink alcohol and worked hard. He was faithful to his wife and had two kids studying in India. Together with his two partners they formed the first travel agency in Bhutan. They started their business in the late 80s when there was hardly any tourism. Ugyen liked to do the office work, but his two partners Kipchue and Kinley loved to trek deep into the mountains, so they were mostly away with clients. Ugyen was the more serious one, Kipchue and Kinley were two handsome men, attracted the interest of many female Western tourists. I once had a lady on a tour who was very interested in Kipchue and another (much older) lady saw it and got jealous. She came to me complaining that the other women should not get involved with Kipchue. I had to laugh, I reassured her that Kipchue was a very experienced guide of 50, a true gentleman and happily married. He would never get involved with clients. That's how I restored harmony between the (older) girls in the group.

CHAPTER 14

WANGMO

When I was in Bhutan, I now stayed with Wangmo and her family. But there was a problem.

Wangmo was a nice young woman when I met her in the Netherlands, but now in Bhutan she seemed to transform into a different person. She ordered me around all the time telling me to pay this, and pay that. The first night I stayed at her family's house, I had horrible nightmares and very strange thoughts were running through my head. I felt that these were not my own thoughts. It was as if something alien was controlling my mind. This may sound a little crazy, but I felt something weird was going on.

Bhutan is known for its living spirituality. Many specialists like monks, lamas, male and female shamans have a lot of esoteric knowledge in working with the forces of nature and their energies. Much time is spent performing rituals to evoke the deities to bring health, luck and protection. This esoteric knowledge can be used for good. But it can also be used for other purposes, to increase wealth, to make people lovesick and to put a spell on someone. As I experienced in the village, there are many *ngejums* and *powas* (shamans) and other practitioners who don't always adhere to the strict practices of Buddhism. Buddhism claims to subdue the dark forces and transform them into forces of light who are then in line with Buddhism and serve all sentient beings for the good. The huge mountains, the magical nature, the pristine forests help to feed the imagination with the notion that there is much more between heaven and earth than we can perceive. The Bhutanese people have huge respect for the forces of nature and worship special places in nature: rocks, lakes, forests, earth and sky, and they have a deep connection to the mysteries of life.

Though the years I have been told that lamas and monks who are trained in the esoteric wisdoms can work with the energies of nature. They can make it rain or cure people who are sick. The many deities who inhabit places in nature can help people but they can also be 'abused'. And what I experienced in Wangmo's house is a strange story.

Wangmo was a short, sturdy woman, who had lived in the Netherlands for many years, married to a tall Dutch man.

Our trip already started strangely because Wangmo confronted me with the fact that she would go to Bhutan a week before me so she could spend some time with her family. It was something I just had to accept. She didn't ask or discuss it with me, although I was paying for her trip. So I flew to Bhutan by myself a week later. I arrived in Paro, the airport town, on a sunny day, and Wangmo was there to pick me up. It was early morning and I had not slept for two nights because of the night flight from Amsterdam to Delhi followed by a very early morning flight from Delhi to Bhutan. I also had jetlag.

Even at the airport, I noticed a change in Wangmo. I had always known her to be friendly and a bit shy. Wangmo was in her early thirties and had two children with her Dutch husband. She had already lived in Holland for many years, but I think deep down she still missed Bhutan. From the airport we drove straight to Thimphu, the capital, a two hour drive. I wanted to go home first to shower and change my clothes, but Wangmo insisted that we first attend some meetings she had arranged. She insisted there was no time for other things. I was jetlagged, hungry, tired and sweaty.

We had meetings with Bhutanese foundations that may have been interested in working with us. But after carefully looking at their proposals, I noticed there was not that much interest because there were only a few foundations, and they were overloaded with work. Bhutan was establishing a civil society, but it still would take many years. Finally, around 6 PM, we went home, and I was exhausted. We stayed with Wangmo's sister Phuntsho, a very kind sweet lady. She gave me a room to myself and I was very grateful for this. I went straight to bed, but I couldn't sleep. For some inexplicable reason, I had a terrible bout of stomach pain. It was a burning sensation, and when I lay down the most horrible thoughts came into my head, very negative thoughts about Wangmo. I thought she would hurt me, betray me. All kinds of crazy dark thoughts ran through my mind. I was a bit overwhelmed by these thoughts, and at first I assumed it was the jet lag affecting me. But as I was lying in my bed, I felt very much awake and conscious of where I was. Those horrible images made me realise that something was wrong. These were not my thoughts.

I almost panicked because I had never experienced anything like this before. It felt as if something had taken over my thoughts, and I had no control over them anymore. This horrible sensation in combination with the stomach pain left me helpless. What could I do? I started to recite mantras, the *gayetry* mantra and om mani ped me hum. After a while I fell asleep yet continued to have frightening nightmares.

Next morning I tried to ignore what happened the night before, but I still felt the pain in my stomach and sensed a heavy cloud over me. In the coming days I tried to stay calm and not show any distress. Together with Wangmo, I went to the office of my local partners, the travel agency. Ugyen's office was in the centre of town on the fourth floor of an office building. Climbing the stairs was like climbing Mount Everest, I always joked. Because of the high altitude of Thimphu, I was always out of breath.

I introduced Wangmo to Ugyen, the CEO of the travel agency, and I was very surprised by Ugyen's comment after Wangmo excused herself to go to the toilet. As soon as she had left the room. Ugyen asked me: "Who is this woman?" I told him she lived in the Netherlands, and she was on the board of the Foundation.

Ugyen replied: "Get rid of her!"

Strangely enough my feeling of discomfort had disappeared as soon as I entered the office of my partners. Ugyen must have known that something was not right because he had never spoken like this to me. The next day we left for Bumthang to do research there and to speak to the officials in the municipality of Jakhar to gather information about the construction of the hotel and school. I tried to defuse the situation by maintaining a friendly disposition towards Wangmo. Although when we came back to Thimphu, I left for Paro as soon as possible. I noticed that when I left Thimphu valley the heavy, unpleasant feeling disappeared and my stomach pain was gone. What could it have been? I started to believe some supernatural forces didn't want me to be with

Wangmo. I cannot tell you why but I had a feeling that she was the one who didn't want me there.

Later I talked to some lamas about this and they said that probably the family of Wangmo was involved in black magic because it really sounded like some spell cast on me. Until today I have no better explanation for this. When I was home I ended my connection with Wangmo. It was obvious that she used the foundation for her own benefit. I tried to find out what the black magic was all about. A lama told me that some Bhutanese families would hire lamas, monks or shamans, who know how to use black magic to increase their wealth or to make people sick. Not much is talked about it to outsiders but to the Bhutanese this is a reality and it is important to protect yourself against it, especially if you are wealthier than others. I remembered the rich farmer in the village who gave rice to the poor couple because he was afraid of the evil eye.

CHAPTER 15

THE POWER OF IGNORANCE

After this very promising start, I struggled to get the project off the ground. It turned out to be very difficult. We had a major financial crisis in Europe. Finding investors was not as easy as I had thought. Even getting donations for the foundation was a real challenge.

My husband is an advisor on sustainable investing strategies in the world of finance. He works in high finance and has a worldwide network of influential, wealthy people. I thought with his access to the financial world, finding investors would be easy. I was very wrong!

I learned a lot. First, a project like this (a startup), in a frontier market, is considered very high risk. Second, I did not have an educational background in hospitality. Third, I am not wealthy myself and could not put €100,000 into the business. These facts posed true challenges.

In a way, it was perhaps a good thing that I was so naive and ignorant, otherwise I would never have started this project. To work for years without money is terrible. I learned that all the platforms to help social entrepreneurs are very political, you need to lobby for yourself and even then it's hard to get support from them. There is always a reason not to help you, among them: "Oh no, we only do investments in Africa." "Oh no, we don't do education, oh no we don't do Bhutan," etc.

There was always a reason they wouldn't invest, although it was stated very clearly on their websites that they would invest exactly in projects like mine. I had to fight my own growing cynicism. I spent three years trying to raise funds for the project, and I didn't get very far. I noticed Bhutan had a strong appeal to certain kinds of people, people who believed Buddhism was some kind of true cause and Bhutan was the promised land, where you went to become enlightened. Because of the difficult access to the country and the commercial Gross National Happiness slogan, many people wanted to jump on board. But they only wanted to jump on board for their own benefit. I felt as if I was rowing a boat and all these people were hanging onto the sides, dragging it down, preventing me from rowing towards my destination. I met many people who wanted to volunteer and help me. But if you are trying to set up a project without money, those people take up too much of your time. Most of the people who want to "help" you have their own agenda. And for quite some time I was so naïve that I thought that their agenda and mine could easily be aligned.

I learned that there was a company in the Netherlands that helped non-profits with fundraising. The gentleman who managed it told me that he had a database with all the foundations in the Netherlands that support non-profits, and funding for education was a big part of it. He told me that I could expect about €40,000 after a first mailing to these foundations.

I thought that this kind of money would be a great help to start the school, so we went ahead. The fundraising company sent out a very professional proposal to their data base. Several months later I only received €3000! The gentleman from the fundraising company was in shock, he had never expected so little money. For him this was a loss too, his own pay consisted of a percentage of the donations given to me. This was in 2010 and the world was in an economic crisis. It turned out that most donor foundations we had approached did fund projects outside the Netherlands. Maybe it would get better as the economy recovered. But of course, as I found out, there is always a reason not to donate.

There are many foundations in the US who talk a lot about the projects they support, but you can't even contact them because they all have "no unsolicited proposals" on their website. Basically you have to know the people who are decision makers in that organisation just to get a chance to submit your proposal. It's all about who you know, a closed circuit of money, power and connections. If this happened in a developing country, it would be called cronyism and perhaps even corruption.

Then I heard that the European Union that has a huge budget to help projects like mine in frontier markets. Many people warned me not to apply for

EU funding because their application forms are so complicated. You need to be a specialist to have a chance. But I thought I had nothing to lose and with the help of a friend from the UK, who is a brilliant writer, we submitted an application. It was all very bureaucratic and I understand that these forms are made for consultants from development agencies who basically only write proposals and reports every day but don't actually work in the field with real people. This was already a huge complaint in Bhutan. All these foreigners who came to 'help' the country basically spent their days in offices writing reports.

One example of this waste of money was a hotel school in Thimphu, built by an European development agency. They spent $10 million to build it, importing all the equipment from Germany and the furniture from Ikea in Sweden. The school was for 50 students, and it was a hotel management school. That sounds very similar to our own project, I thought. I must find out.

When I went there to see what they were doing, I was shocked. A lot of the kitchen equipment was broken, and nobody knew how to fix it. Overall the place looked dirty and neglected. What a waste!

To make sure that my EU application met the deadline, I decided to deliver it to the Brussels office myself by train. I handed the envelope to a receptionist who told me he would take care of it. A week later I received an email that they had received my application but it didn't have a date stamp on the envelope, so they didn't know if I had sent it in on time! I told them I had handed it over myself at their office. But that was not good enough, I now had to prove that I actually did what someone in their office should have recorded. I had to send them my train ticket to Brussels as proof. What madness!

Of course we didn't get the grant, we didn't tick all the boxes apparently. I learned that a few years earlier a project in Bhutan was heavily funded by the EU. However, this project was actually a scam, but the people who wrote the proposal were very good consultants.

There are many organisations worldwide who claim to help social entrepreneurs with projects in non-Western countries, but I learned that all is not as it seems. Many of them just don't support start-ups, and all of them have their own agenda.

For example I contacted the Dutch organisation Stichting Action, whose marketing material claims to support projects exactly like mine. Of course they didn't wanted to support my project. They said it didn't fit, but I met all the requirements. Then there was Echoing Green, who claim to support social entrepreneurs, also a waste of time. I asked people from Ashoka, who told me they didn't support projects in Bhutan. I even tried to become a B-Corp member, but I realised that they want you to pay a hefty monthly membership fee, and there is not really an upside for start-up entrepreneurs. The sad thing is that clubs like B-Corp are not transparent themselves.

I talked to banks, even to a Swiss bank that had a client, a very rich Nepalese entrepreneur, who wanted to invest in hotels in Bhutan, but it turned out he only wanted to have access to land. Later I learned that this Nepalese company had a very bad reputation in all of South Asia.

Then one day a man from Norway contacted me. He wanted to meet me to talk about the Bhutan project.

He claimed to be an investor and invited me to lunch, one that I had to pay for myself. His promise was a collaboration with a hotel school project in Myanmar. He would invest, so we could grow and establish a true quality hotel school, build hotels and even start a school for arts and crafts. This man worked with very wealthy Norwegian women, who had helped a Burmese entrepreneur set up a hotel and school in Inle Lake.

Again I was so happy, I thought this was a way forward towards my objective, and we could build up the business together. But it turned out to be all lies. I called one of the wealthy women in Norway to ask how we would move forward, and she told me she was not interested in investing in the project. The Myanmar project was very different from the way it had been presented. She had simply lent money to the Burmese entrepreneur and he was paying it back. Another disappointment, another waste of time for me.

THE CELLIST

While I was back in the Netherlands, working on the foundation and the hotel funding, sending out the first draft business plan and exploring funding and investors, I got a call from a friend, the director of a conservatorium here. He invited me for dinner, so I could meet a cellist friend of his who wanted to do a project in Bhutan. I was not too keen on meeting this person because I was worried that it would be another case of someone who was very attracted to Bhutan for their own reasons, not so much to help the foundation but to get access to the country without paying the $250 per day. But my friend insisted.

We met in a nice restaurant and Maria, the cellist, was at first sight a very charming American lady. She wanted to do a Western classical music project in Bhutan.

"I think the world would benefit more if Bhutanese music was preserved and celebrated. Nobody expects a Bhutanese cellist to play Bach, many people around the world already do that. But classical Bhutanese music is rare and very precious and in danger of being lost."

"The Bhutanese do not have music", the American cellist said.

I was shocked. I should have listened to my intuition.

She told me her plan was to bring string instruments to Bhutan and give children access to classical music. Although I wasn't convinced, I told her I could help her with setting up a foundation.

Maria suggested that I should go meet Dechen, the lady who was in charge of running the music school, when I was next in Bhutan. This way I could see the school for myself. Soon after this meeting I was going on one of my trips to Bhutan and visited the music school. It made a good impression on me. But they didn't have a lot of instruments, just a piano and some guitars.

I asked around about Western classical music in Bhutan. Most people told me that young Bhutanese are not familiar with western classical music, they don't hear it at home and they don't have the discipline to practice the violin or the cello, let alone being able to buy an instrument like that.

Nevertheless, I helped Maria set up her foundation. I arranged a trip for us, paid for by my travel agency partners, to Bhutan. I thought it would be great to arrange a music trip to Bhutan, accompanying the cellist who would perform in all the major towns, and we could invite local Bhutanese musicians to play together with her. This would be unique. I talked to my Dutch travel agents, and they liked the idea and started to sell the trip to their clients. So Marie and I went to Bhutan to inspect all the places she could perform and meet the local musicians.

Maria was a real cello virtuoso and famous for her very unusual avant-garde music. I went to several of her concerts, and I must admit her music was magical. I was looking forward to the trip to Bhutan with her. Maria was very smart and had a great sense of humour, but she also had days when she acted strangely and was very distant. I didn't think much of it, explaining it as the normal mood swings of an artist.

But when we arrived in Thimphu, I saw a very different side of Maria who had been so charming in

Amsterdam. It was almost like what had happened with Wangmo. What was going on? What did this country do to people?

It seemed Maria became jealous of me. She said: "All the people here love you." After the first day in the capital I was not allowed to come with her to her meetings with Bhutanese musicians and other people vital for the music trip. I was not allowed to talk to her, although she slept in the room next to me. I had to send her an email first to ask her if *la grande dame* would grant me an audience of a minute to talk to her. One moment she was the nicest person on the planet, the next moment she was absolutely horrible. In the Netherlands she had asked me to be on the board of her foundation and as a board member it would have been very normal to be with her when we had meetings with the Bhutanese music institutions.

But in Bhutan she said: "I am the face of the foundation, and I want to be the most important person."

"Of course you are the musician," I said, "and it's your foundation, but as a board member I can help you."

But no, I had to disappear, she only wanted me when she needed something. Friends back in the Netherlands urged me to get out of this project! But this was easier said than done. We were travelling to central Bhutan to prepare for the music trip. I was the one who had all arranged that. I couldn't just forget about it, so I had to endure the trip. I thought, never again! I'll never go to Bhutan again with people who don't pay for their own trip and who only want something for themselves. I felt I needed to protect myself. In the future people could hire me, and pay for my services.

I felt that I had made the same mistake with Wangmo and now with Maria. I had hoped to have good cooperation with both of them, to have mutual respect and to help each other to make the project a success.

How wonderful it would be to have a collaboration between a music school and a hotel school. We could have organised events together, and the students at the hotel school, who were usually kids who had grown up with few privileges, could learn about music, while the musicians learned about food and hospitality. Wangmo, who lived in the Netherlands, could have been a strong part of the hotel school, like a brand ambassador. This was my hope and vision. But I learned that I trusted people too quickly, a very important lesson for the future.

Away from Thimphu, Maria behaved in a more civilised manner, but it was obvious that she was a diva. One day she didn't want to talk to me and avoided me. The next day she was as sweet as could be and asked me to go for a walk in the countryside with her, as if nothing had happened. Back in Amsterdam I withdrew from her foundation. She said she couldn't understand it. I tried to explain that her behaviour in Bhutan was not acceptable, and she said she didn't know what I was talking about. Later I learned that she really had psychological problems.

THE BARONESS

Short after Maria, another very colourful person came into my life, a German baroness who was an investor and was interested in the hotel in Bhutan. She was a bit unusual as well, she called her investment firm "Capital in Love". For her it was important to bring the Eros aspect into investing, she said, and she was looking for investments that were all about love, sensuality and beauty. She had a blog called "Investment Poetry".

My love for Bhutan was a lot more real, a love that had grown in contact with real people and real experiences.

It was obvious she was not serious about investing, she was bored and wanted to learn more about my project. This is something I learned too. Many investors tell you they are interested but in the end they just want to get information from you. My husband warned me about them.

Now I could reflect on how blissful my life was while working on my Ph.D. Now, as an entrepreneur, I started to learn about the dark side of the world, the world of money and power. The world of ego! Even with my small project, I got to know how the real world operates. Seemingly I was not yet up to the challenges and pitfalls it presented.

CHAPTER 16

PAOLO TO THE RESCUE AND A LEADERSHIP PROJECT

But then one day, my husband and I were invited to stay at a private villa in Sardinia, Italy. The host, Paolo, was an Italian nobleman, who was very hospitable and charming. He looked just like the late actor, Gregory Peck. Paolo invited us to his beautiful estate near the Costa Esmeralda, with several villas and a swimming pool, horse stables, tennis courts, all set in a beautiful landscape. Such a joy to spend a week there. Eight other guests from the Italian corporate world were invited. The purpose of this meeting was to inspire each other and to share experiences in the field of sustainable impact investing and social entrepreneurship. All of us were working on projects that were aiming to make a positive impact on the world.

I presented my project of a for-profit culturally authentic eco-lodge and non-profit school. Paolo loved it. He had been to Bhutan, so he knew the country. During our stay at his estate he didn't say much, only that my project was fabulous. So we went home and I continued the struggle to find investors.

A new member was coming onto the board of the foundation. This member had lived in Bhutan for six years, and she introduced me to a very accomplished Bhutanese lady Mrs Phuntsho who became the counterpart of our foundation in Bhutan for the next phase of the project.

We wanted to start training young unemployed girls and boys in Bhutan and see how we could help them. We decided to organise a personal leadership program to help them find their passion and their talents. Most of them had never thought about this.

I started to raise funding for it, but it was hard. But then, we received a very generous donation from a lady from Hong Kong! It meant that we could put on a full week of training for 50 girls and boys in a hotel in Bumthang. I was so happy. I felt that this donation was a very welcome proof of trust.

This personal leadership program was fantastic! Mrs Phuntsho arranged the hotel, and for most of the 50 young people it was the first time they themselves could stay for a week in a hotel where tourists stayed for $250 a night. Of course Mrs Phuntsho was a tough negotiator, and we got the venue very cheaply. The owner liked what we were doing and wanted to help us. I loved being with the young Bhutanese and to see how much they needed some attention and guidance. They were all good kids between 16 and 22, and they also helped each other. But they told heart-breaking stories. When we handed out forms to be filled in, one question was "what makes you happy?" One boy wrote "not to be hungry". Several young people had endured domestic violence and poverty. But most of all there was a lack of guidance from their parents. Many young people in Bhutan have parents who are still traditional farmers and are illiterate. They put tremendous pressure on their children, wanting them to find good white collar jobs because they had the chance to study. Being a farmer is traditionally regarded as low status, because as a farmer you kill a lot of bugs and worms while ploughing. This is bad for your karma, while being a civil servant and sitting at a desk is regarded as a much better job with better status.

The ideas that young people in Bhutan have about a possible career are not very realistic. But how can they have a realistic view if they don't have role models or guidance from parents or other people? For example, all the students wanted to be "successful business people", but when I asked them what a successful business man or woman was, they looked at me with blank faces, they had no idea!

When we asked them what they want to do in the future, most of them told me they wanted to start a travel agency, because this is the only thing they know. But they forget that there are already more than 1,000 travel agencies in Bhutan and there are only a 100,000 clients per year. The top ten travel agencies in Bhutan deal with the majority of these clients. It's not very realistic to start a new travel agency with no knowledge and connections outside Bhutan to attract clients.

So we explained to them that it would be good to first determine what your passions are, what you like to do, what makes you happy. They had never thought about that. We did all kinds of activities to help them find their purpose and give them guidance for their future.

Just the fact that they could stay in a hotel for a whole week, like a tourist, made them so happy. What amazed me so much was that the young people were very caring towards each other. We were very happy to learn that we helped at least ten youngsters to find their destiny, and they found jobs and training for their future. We hoped to do a follow up week but we lacked the funding. 2013 was a very tough year. Fundraising was on hold. In the Netherlands, most donors were, again, only giving donations to projects in the Netherlands. So I had to revise my strategy.

PAOLO IN BHUTAN

Then one day, Paolo, the host of the week in Sardinia, contacted me and told me he would like to invest in my project. Specifically, he wanted to help me get the hotel project off the ground.

This was terrific news. Paolo was a very accomplished businessman. With him on board, things started to fly. We went to Bhutan together and, fortunately, this trip went well. We had meetings with the FDI, the Foreign Direct Investment office, visited the prospective locations, and Paolo met our local partners, Mr Ugyen and his associates.

Paolo is a seasoned financier, the former CEO of large corporations and a banker. He comes from an aristocratic Italian background and that energy was all around him. It was interesting to see his interactions with the Bhutanese men, for example just the way Paolo entered the office of the ministry of economic affairs. He had a great personal presence and the civil servants saw it and regarded him with a level of respect that they never showed me. They were obviously impressed. I thought: Aha, this is how it works in the male world! This is what women face at high levels in politics and the corporate world.

There was mutual respect, but also a very subtle ego fight, especially with the bureaucrats, because they drove Paolo crazy. I noticed that Paolo was used to giving orders not filling in forms. But now he didn't have a PA, so he had to do it himself. Watching him, I could see clearly that we still live in a man's world, and it's so much easier for men to get things done and to be taken seriously. Although men also bend the truth a lot and always brag about things, something that women don't do as much.

During our last evening in Bhutan I visited a friend who has a large hotel in Paro. It was built in the late 1970s when Bhutan was still very much closed to the outside world. The hotel had 20 rooms, a restaurant, conference room, a kitchen and a lot of land around it. It was in a very bad state, but the owner was willing to rent the whole building to use as a campus and training facility for the school. We agreed to rent it for a good price.

After we were back in Europe we started to professionalise the whole project.

From now on I was no longer alone and everything changed. Paolo made sure that we worked with professionals with a track record to make sure the project was successful.

Before I was too naïve and too enthusiastic about having people on the board of my project. It turned out that most of the people that I had chosen to work with were not suitable. Because I had no money, I was grateful that people were willing to help me without upfront payment. This was also the main reason why I wasted so much time. I was too trusting, and I was also desperate for someone to help me, a bad combination for starting a project.

The architect that I had chosen was a well-known architect who specialised in ecological architecture. But he didn't have any experience of building in mountains and had no track record of building hotels. He created a design for our hotel but Paolo saw immediately that it wouldn't work. I had to let him go, and he was furious. The architect wanted to be on this project because of Bhutan, and because he was hoping to make a name for himself. In the end this architect sent me a bill for €30,000. I was very grateful to the treasurer of the foundation, who helped me to avoid any more mistakes like that in the future.

The search for the right architect continued. When a mutual friend introduced Miranda, I was a bit sceptical at first. She was another person who talked a lot about her connections with the royals in Bhutan. This was not the route I wanted to go down, particularly after my previous experiences. I wanted to be independent and with work with ordinary local people like my Bhutanese colleagues and partners. But Paolo wanted to give her a try, and since she lived in Switzerland, not so far from another one of Paolo's properties, they were able to meet up. Paolo was very happy with Miranda and it seemed she was the right person to work with us. She had a lot of construction experience in frontier markets and in mountain areas. She also specialised in hotels. Her passion was cultural authenticity. She was the right architect.

CHAPTER 17

THE POWER OF THE RIGHT TEAM

A fter our first group meeting in Switzerland at Paolo's house, we decided to take a trip to Bhutan with all the players.

In Switzerland, Miranda the architect, Mark, a Dutch financial expert, Martin, a financial hotel specialist Francis, the son of a very wealthy Swiss man with a background in hotel education, and Paolo's daughter, a communication specialist, came together for a long weekend to prepare all the work. Paolo's chalet was a picturesque wooden apartment in the old town of Verbiers. Paolo himself again exuded the typical Italian warmth and hospitality. Miranda, Mark and I stayed in Paolo's chalet. It was so cosy with its Swiss style woodstove and its wonderful view onto the mountain peaks of the Alps. With a little imagination we could have pictured ourselves in Bhutan, the smoke from the open wood fire, the thin air and the amazing view of the snow peaks. There are a lot of similarities between Switzerland and Bhutan. They are both mountain people, Bhutanese houses look like Swiss chalets and the Bhutanese national dish is melted cheese with chillies, similar to the Swiss fondue, only much spicier.

It felt very peculiar for me to have all these strange people come together and talk about my project as if they owned it. I had been working on it for several years on my own, and all these complete strangers talking about it started to worry me.

I realised that I was concerned about others taking over my project. This was a very scary feeling. I also wasn't used to the arrogant attitude of some of these people. I needed to be assertive and claim my place.

So many people warn you that when you start a project like mine there is always a chance that some else will take over, especially when you get investors on board. But on the other hand, if I wanted to move on with the project I had to let other people in. It's an internal conflict that can never be completely resolved, but I had to get on with it.

Paolo decided that we needed professional trainers for the school and hired a young man, a son of a friend of his. His name was Francis, and he would work together with Adam, the main trainer we hired for the hotel school. Adam was a hotel specialist and had worked with a professor from the Lausanne hotel school in setting up hotel schools in developing countries.

The problem with Francis started with the first trip to Bhutan that we planned that weekend. If you want to visit Bhutan you need a visa and someone needs to invite you, in this case it would be Mrs Phuntsho through the ministry of labour.

But Francis decided to go to Bhutan without first consulting us. He just booked his tickets. Paolo and Francis had no idea how difficult it was to get him a visa at the last moment. Fortunately, Mrs Phuntsho was able to arrange a free visa for him. He could stay for a month.

Our team, Miranda, Paolo, and myself, were going to meet Francis in Bhutan and would spend a week together travelling to Bumthang. The trip was set for late April 2014.

We decided we would all stay together at Mr Pem's hotel because we wanted to rent it to become our school and training hotel. I had talked to Mr Pem, and we agreed on a reasonable rent for the old hotel. We needed to completely renovate it because the whole place was falling apart.

Anybody who travelled to India in the 70s or 80s knows what I am talking about. The bathrooms were a complete disaster. The faucets didn't work, most of the time there was no water. Or there was only boiling hot water or only cold water, and the water poured out from everywhere except the faucets. The rooms had never been cleaned properly. The whole place was old, ugly and dirty according to Western standards. After a few days staying with Mr. Pem, we hired a bus to go to Bumthang to see the land there. It was a 12 hour trip, a long drive along a small mountain road. The maximum driving speed was 40 km per hour, and most of the time even slower because some of these roads are very bad. I asked Francis if he had been travelling in Bhutan during the three weeks he had been there, and to my surprise he told me he had not, he had been sleeping most of the time. I heard from my Bhutanese friends in Paro that they had tried to socialise with him but he was a bit strange. He didn't do any of the work Adam had asked him to do to prepare for the set-up of the school.

Our trip to Bumthang went well, Miranda saw the land and she liked it very much. Of course, for a luxury hotel, the location is absolutely vital. Back in Paro it was obvious that Francis was not the right person for the job.

One day before we had to leave Bhutan, we had a meeting with Mr Pem to talk about the rental. To our shock, Mr Pem suddenly decided to increase the rent by a hundred percent. We had already agreed on a reasonable rent, and we would renovate his hotel to the standard of a proper 3 star hotel. Mr Pem would get a fully renovated hotel and a hospitality school thrown into his lap, and now he wanted even more! We were in shock. Paolo was freaking out.

"What can we do now?" he said, "this will set us back a year"!

Then I remembered my friend Choden, who had

told me about a friend with a hotel in Paro that he wanted to rent out. It was a newer hotel and in better shape than Mr. Pem's hotel. So we decided to call him, and he invited us to come and look at his place. We went immediately. The hotel really was much nicer than Mr Pem's. Only the bathrooms were in the same broken-down style. But the rooms were nice and clean. The owner, Ms Karma, was the lady of the house, a warm, kind woman with a beautiful face and a friendly smile full of red teeth because of the many betel nuts she loved to chew. She was a passionate farmer too and grew all her crops organically. The whole family was made up of very kind people, father Jigme, mother Karma, two sons and one daughter. They agreed to rent us their hotel and besides that, they wanted to be involved in setting up the school. The next day I went to the hotel to present a memorandum of understanding (MOU) to Ms Karma, the owner of the hotel. She invited us to a delicious lunch and told us she could not sign the MOU today because it was a Wednesday and Wednesday was not a lucky day for her. Her astrologer had advised her never to sign any papers on a Wednesday. So she didn't. But we would have a problem because the next day I had to fly out early in the morning. She assured me that she would come to my hotel as early as necessary to sign the papers, and she did.

Now that we had rented this new hotel, the project had become real and Paolo and I were very excited. I was also a very nervous now. Partly because I was a bit worried about the way Paolo worked, he just decided important matters without conferring, and he often didn't really have a plan. And I also felt overwhelmed by the enormity of the situation. My project was no longer just on paper and in my head. It was happening.

In November 2014 we finally started the preparations for the school.

We had hired Adam from the Ecole Hotelier de Lausanne and Anton from the Hague Hotel School, and we started to adapt the hotel that we had rented to become a school. Adam, the young Swiss man, skinny with spiky blond hair was very serious and dedicated. In addition, he also had a great sense of humour. He had worked in many countries, setting up hotel schools from scratch. The young Dutch man, Anton, was tall and more playful and enthusiastic.

He reminded me of a puppy dog, always cheerful and playful. They hadn't met before the job started, so I hoped they would get on with each other since they would have to stay and work in the hotel together for a year.

On their first day, the two young men met Mr. Jigme, the owner of the hotel that we rented. Mr. Jigme had intelligent eyes in a wrinkled face, wrinkled from a lifetime of smiling. His mouth was red from years of chewing betel nut. Mr. Jigme was from an old family from Paro and full of surprises. A simple, friendly man, full of laughter, observant, and smart. Most of the time he just wore old tracksuit pants and an old jacket. But he had many different layers of knowledge and empathy, and he had a seemingly never-ending supply of connections in Bhutan. We struck gold by finding him.

Before I got to know Jigme I had worked with Mrs Phuntsho, a very accomplished lady, but she was overburdened and although she wanted to do the project with me she couldn't find the time. So the local partners changed again.

Mr Jigme's home was an ancient old Paro farm

house, with amazing altar rooms full of ancient old Buddha statues and holy books, *sutras* that only special monks can recite. Jigme's family is a very interesting mixture of ancient old Bhutanese, who keep the tradition alive, fused with modern lifestyle in a very natural way. Jigme's children are educated. His oldest son is an engineer and Jigme worked for a bank before he retired. His youngest daughter is studying to be a psychologist, a new profession in Bhutan. Jigme also has a vast network of cousins, nieces and nephews in powerful positions who helped us with everything. When I wasn't feeling well, Jigme took me to his niece who was a doctor, who took good care of me. When we needed a lawyer to draft the papers for the institute, of course Jigme had a cousin, who was an excellent lawyer. When I wanted to consult an astrologer, Jigme took me to a high lama, his neighbour, who was famous throughout the country because of his spiritual powers. He even identified important *tulkus* (reincarnated Buddhist teachers of important lineages) in Bhutan. I consulted him in his house full of Buddha statues and a huge altar. I saw that the lama used a bell that looked very old, it turned out be the bell used by guru Rinpoche in the seventh century. I was sitting on a chair in his cramped room filled with *thankhas* (religious paintings), holy books, and many Buddha statues. Before he started to calculate my horoscope, he burned incense and recited mantras. His prediction was a bit strange, because he did not say much, only that I should avoid eating meat, wearing black on a Monday and sitting in a green car because I could have an accident. After our meeting the lama invited me to his *lhakhang* (temple) to show me a *terton*, a treasure hidden by guru Rinpoche in the seventh century. But sadly I never made it to this temple.

CHAPTER 18

MY BEAUTIFUL SCHOOL

S o here I was in Paro with two young, eager Western boys and Jigme's family. It turned out that Jigme had even more family to share, this time a nephew, Karma, who started a hotel all by himself, with no experience. He had built a 58 room hotel from scratch and he had done a very good job. He invited us for lunch and asked us for help with his kitchen and his spa. We decided to work together. He needed experts to advise him on how to improve things on a professional level, and we needed advice on where to buy good materials and where to find good workman.

Karma introduced us to a good engineer. Wonderful material and building products are available in Bhutan, for example tiles and faucets, but there is an overall lack of skilled tradesmen and craftsmen. To have a bathroom installed professionally is almost like building the Taj Mahal. Most of the hotels have their bathrooms done by Indian workmen from West Bengal, and unfortunately the result often is that nothing works and every tile on the wall is crooked. The faucets are installed in such a way that the water will flow everywhere except into the sink. Showers don't work, and hot water comes out of the cold-water faucet and the cold water pours out of the hot-water faucet.

The next major step was to buy the equipment. We found out that there was a shop in Thimphu that sold professional kitchen supplies and a shop that sold bathrooms. We also went on an expedition to Phuntsholing, the border town with India where all the goods from India are sold at a cheaper price. Later we learned from Karma who had bought some of the

Indian made kitchen equipment, an oven and a fridge, that they all stopped working after a few months. So maybe it might be better to buy the goods from Bangkok, Thailand, as so many Bhutanese do with the large screen TVs they take on their flights back to the kingdom.

To promote our project we organised a Bhutanese evening for two Swiss tourist groups. We had a bonfire, a cultural programme and traditional Bhutanese food in our hotel and school while it was still under construction.

To make the evening even more special I asked Mr Jigme's family to prepare typical food from the different regions of Bhutan. Momos were served, a Bhutanese and Tibetan dish, dumplings with different fillings, like beef, pork or cheese. Yak meat was served, and the national Bhutanese dish *ema datsi*, melted cottage cheese with lots of chillies. The Bhutanese eat chillies as vegetables, and they can be fiercely hot, but for the tourists they adjusted the dishes.

The Swiss group arrived around 7 PM to a bonfire in the middle of the courtyard. It always surprises me how lost Western tourists look in Bhutan. This

French Swiss group all looked a bit uncomfortable and lost too, but the evening went very well. Jigme's family presented the group with drinks and snacks and people started to relax. After dinner a cultural group sang songs and performed traditional dances from the different regions of Bhutan. I often don't like these displays just for tourists but in Bhutan it is very common to have cultural dance performances when you have a party, including government functions. I like this tradition because it preserves the heritage and gives the performers an income.

To determine our real budget, we had to make an inventory of what we already had and what we still needed. The kitchen and bathrooms were in very bad shape. We decided to tear everything out. In many places in Bhutan, people just start hotels with no knowledge whatsoever, they try to provide a good service that is based on the warm hospitality that the Bhutanese have in their culture. But to run a 13-room hotel with a restaurant is a different story.

Our inventory revealed that, basically, we had to buy everything new. While the old cutlery, china and glasses could be used for the students, we needed new professional china for the hotel. Now the big challenge was where to buy it. We needed the lowest price with the best quality. A lot of equipment is imported from Bangkok, this is good quality but it has a higher price and needs to be shipped to Bhutan via Kolkata and then on a truck up into the Himalayas. This can take a month. To buy in India means cheap prices but inferior quality, especially when it comes to kitchen equipment. It was a big quest to find out what would be our best plan of action. We needed quotations from everywhere. But first we needed to go to the border towns of Jagoan in India and Phuntcholing in Bhutan. The Bordertown Jagoan is the big shopping town for the Bhutanese. Because it is in India and the goods don't have to be transported on trucks up the mountains of Bhutan, all the prices are much lower and there is much more choice in the shops than in the capital Thimphu

Adam, Anton and I drove to Phuntcholing to do the shopping. This trip was a real adventure. Driving down from the Himalayas to the Indian plains is a spectacular journey. We descended from an altitude of 2,700 metres to 300 metres above sea level. I have travelled on this road many times as a guide and I love it. The small winding road South follows the *'duars'* as the rivers that flow out of the Himalayas into India were called during the time of British rule, the 'doors' to the majestic mountains. The road is carved into mountains that are halfway hidden in the clouds. We drove in Mr. Jigme's Hilux four-wheel drive with some nice pop music on the radio.

"Wow, this landscape reminds me of Jurassic Park," said Anton, looking out of the window. "I wouldn't be surprised to see a real living dinosaur at the next corner."

"Yes," I said, "it really looks that way."

Halfway down our bumpy road we made a stop at an India army camp that had a small restaurant serving delicious masala dosa, a crispy pancake with curried potatoes, and samosas. All three of us realised what a gigantic task it must have been making this road. Until the mid-1960s, people had to walk from the border of India for five days through a thick malaria-infested jungle to get to the capital Thimphu.

Around 4 PM we arrived in Phuntcholing and enjoyed the warm humid air of the subtropical environment. I cannot think of a place with a greater contrast than the twin border towns of Phuntcholing in Bhutan and Jagoan in India, joined by a big Bhutanese entrance gate. The Bhutanese side is clean and quiet, with neat little shops and many restaurants-cum-bars in which women and men sit and enjoy a cold beer. On the other side of the gate is the chaos of India, on the streets you see mainly men, cows, rikshas, dirt and dust, and you hear the non-stop honking of trucks and cars. The road is one big garbage dump and hardly paved. The overall smell is dust and urine from humans and cows.

To me Jagoan could be the ugliest town in India. Because of the damp climate the buildings look like the remains of a nuclear explosion, covered in mildew, grey and in a state of despair. A sharp contrast with the traditional building style of the Bhutanese houses just across the border that is pleasing to the eye. I love India and there are many places in India that are just as beautiful as Bhutan. But India is a huge continent and Jagoan is a border city in West Bengal, one of the poorest states in India, and it shows. Roads are badly maintained and close to Jagoan there are big tea plantations that use bonded labour. There is also a lot of political unrest in the region. Not an easy place to be.

We checked into a hotel on the Bhutanese side and ordered a nice Indian meal. The next day we went to review the prices of the items we need for the hotel and school.

After a night full of mosquito bites and a nice Indian breakfast, we went to go shopping on the Indian side. First we checked bathroom items and tiles. Most of the shopkeepers in Jagoan are Marwaris, very accomplished business people who came from Hariyana and Rajasthan a long time ago and settled in Sikkim and West Bengal to do business in the Himalayan regions. A very pleasant experience for me was the respect the shop owners showed me, an older woman. They were very polite to me and addressed all their questions to me, not so much to the boys. What a difference to Western cultures! In all my travels in India, I am always surprised by the Indian genius of making something out of nothing. Even their skill to sell you something you absolutely don't need is pure art. We spent all day in shops to select what we needed for the school and to find out all the prices so we could create a realistic budget. So, this time round, we didn't purchase anything. After two days we went back to Paro and it was time for me to fly back home. The boys would stay behind and supervise the renovation of the hotel and start the set-up of the school.

CHAPTER 19

THE FOUNDER FINDS
THE FUNDS

N ow we had a school, Paolo had put in the seed money and that made it much easier for me to raise money. But although Paolo himself was a wealthy man and had very wealthy friends, for him it was difficult to do any fundraising. He said he couldn't ask his friends to support the foundation and the school. He trusted me to bring in a lot of donations. Which I did later on.

I started to send out proposals, talked to friends and, with the school a real live project now, money did come in! We also received larger amounts from foundations in the Netherlands and outside the Netherlands. Suddenly there was enough money to start the school and pay for everything. Of course there was never enough but with Mr Jigme's support, talking to the ministry of labour of Bhutan (they also helped financially) we would be able to run the school well. I have to say I just hated fundraising, but after a while, particularly if you are at last successful, it becomes a sport. I always felt like I was begging for money, but you also can turn it around and see it as presenting people with a great project. Many foundations are looking for good projects to give money to, so in a way you are helping them to fulfil their mission. This attitude makes it much easier to raise funds because you maintain your power. You are offering the world something great.

One evening on my next trip to Bhutan we were sitting in the little wooden shack that would become a bar when the school and hotel was up and running. Mr. Jigme came to have a chat with us. He told us about 'the captain'. "What captain?" I asked him. He told me that he was renting out part of his house to a captain from Drukair. This captain was a very experienced pilot of Indian descent. Only specially trained pilots can fly for a Bhutanese airline because of the special conditions of the landing strips. Paro airport in Bhutan has the most dangerous landing strip in the world because the valley is so narrow, and there can be strong winds that make it difficult to land. There is no radar and there are only visual landing conditions. Of course those dangerous conditions are a dream for die-hard pilots.

Jigme told us about this captain and told us he was coming for a drink to meet us.

A bit later Tashi, Jigme's son knocked at our door and he brought the captain with him. He was a jolly gentleman with a very British accent because he had lived and studied in England. I guessed he must be in his 40s and he entertained us all evening. The captain invited me to the cockpit, when he was on duty, the next time I had to fly Drukair. Gosh I would love to experience this. He said how wonderful it was to be able to invite friends into the cockpit, this is no longer possible almost everywhere else in the world.

Maybe if I can ever go to Bhutan again, I'll fly there in the gallant captain's cockpit.

We had a wonderful evening and agreed that we would have dinner together the next day in Paro's best restaurant and have Aum Lalita's famous buttered chicken. Aum Lalita is originally from Sikkim and she is a Lepcha, the indigenous people of Sikkim. Not much is known about these gentle, nature loving people. Sadly enough there are only about 30,000 Lepcha left in Sikkim and in the Darjeeling area. Most Lepcha intermarried with Nepalese and Bhutia, of Tibetan descent. They migrated to Sikkim over the centuries, many fleeing the wars of the Buddhist sects between the fifteenth and eighteenth century in Tibet.

Aum Lalita's restaurant is in the middle of Paro town on the second floor above a bank. The walls are panelled with wood and there are six tables. It has a cosy feel, many local Bhutanese eat here. In addition to the buttered chicken I ordered another one of Aum Lolita's specialities, black pork. I was curious what that would be, and we were pleasantly surprised. It was pork belly marinated in many spices and soy sauce, cooked for hours and roasted. The result was a fragrant meat dish, almost black but very delicious.

After dinner we decided to have a nightcap at Karma's hotel. Karma was Mr Jigme's nephew, an interesting and handsome man in his 40, married to a Bhutanese actress who owns a small shop in the village of Bongde where our school is. Karma was the nephew who had built a 58 room hotel from scratch. He did an amazing job without any experience. The rooms of his hotel are comfortable and well designed. The lobby and dining room are perhaps a little too big to make them cosy. But this is definitely one of the best 100% Bhutanese hotels. It also had a great bar with Bhutanese draft beer, unique in the country.

In the bar, we started a conversation about Bhutan and India. India, Bhutan's giant neighbour is always a hot topic because Bhutan is so dependent on India.

But culturally the countries are very different, and there is often a lot of tension. We were enjoying a lively discussion and suddenly a British gentleman sitting alone in the bar reading a book started to address the captain with his own views on India. According to him, the cause of all the problems in India was the size of its population. Here we go again, I thought. Maybe he thinks that India is still the jewel in the crown of the British Empire, but these times are over. We agreed to disagree with the British gentleman and decided to call it a night. We went home – yes, the hotel school was now 'home' to us – for a good night's sleep under the stars of the Himalayan skies. I dreamed that night that I was sitting next to the captain in the cockpit of his plane and flying over the mountain tops of the Himalayas.

Karma asked me if I could help him with his spa, he had built a very nice spa in his hotel but he didn't have well trained masseuses. I told him that I could help him to find a good experienced massage teacher from the Netherlands if he would pay travel and board for her. I found him an older lady in the Netherlands, who was a very experienced massage therapist, very funny and eccentric. She went to Bhutan for three months and did a great job training the young girls from the spa. I heard that they all loved her, and she loved it there as well. And this is one of the things that I love so much about Bhutan, with so little you can do so much.

Saturday night, and the boys and I were invited by my dear friend Sonam. Sonam is the sister of Dorji, my last and best translator 25 years ago in the village, the one who saved my research after all the others had run away, from the poverty and from Aum Zam, the female shaman. Sonam stayed with me in my home in Amsterdam for three months. I helped her to get an internship in Amsterdam with an architect. She went on to study architecture in India. Sonam is a wonderful girl with a beautiful smile, and very smart. She invited us for a night out in Thimphu. Nightlife in Thimphu was very new to me because I am an early sleeper, and I never made it to the late bars. I was warned by young Bhutanese guys to be careful, they said that some bars can be dangerous, you can be robbed there, and there are even gangs and knife fights. This totally contradicted the Gross National

Happiness slogan that the government tries to sell to the world.

In the end, Bhutan is just a country like all others.

I suppose, when I was able to that conclusion, the long honeymoon period was finally over. But maybe a more mature, more realistic relationship was forming, one that had been growing for a long time. I loved Bhutan now with the intimate knowledge of a long-term partner, and a lifelong friend. I had outgrown some of my illusions and embraced the country as it really was.

The boys and I left for Thimphu by taxi, a two-hour drive. Thimphu is maybe the only capital city in the world without a MacDonald's or a KFC, without traffic lights, and hardly any ugly billboards. Thimphu is maybe the only capital where the streets are stained red with smelly betel nut juice and, sadly, a lot of garbage.

Sonam came to pick us up from our hotel (we rented a room for one night in a cheap guesthouse) because driving back to Paro late at night was not possible. She took us to a new restaurant in the centre of town. Four of her friends were already there, two ladies and two men, very intelligent, friendly young people in their late 20s. We ordered beer and snacks, Bhutanese chicken wings, *ema datshi* and of course cheese *momos*. Adam is normally a very quiet and serious person, but when he gets in the right mood, he is one of the funniest people I know. He could almost be like a stand-up comedian. I told him that in the old days the rank of a Bhutanese man could be seen by the size of the white sleeves he wore with his *gho*. The higher the rank, the wider the sleeves.

Adam immediately reacted with a funny face: "Oh then I will wear sleeves that go up all the way to under my armpits," he said, "that way I will be very important."

We enjoyed our food and good conversation and after dinner we went to a karaoke bar. Karaoke is immensely popular in Bhutan now, and there are many little bars where you can sing your heart out. This bar was a big bar with a full stage. We were the first there, so we took over the stage as more friends of Sonam joined us. Many Bhutanese pop songs were played and pretty girls were singing. Bhutanese pop songs are strongly influenced by Hindi pop, with high pitched voices and sugary sweet lyrics, not very much appreciated by Western standards. Of course the sweet music was accompanied by a lightshow that featured all the colours of the rainbow and plenty of bling. Around 1 AM I had enough and went back to my hotel in Thimphu. The boys stayed on to enjoy the nightlife to its fullest. Walking to my hotel, I felt a scary atmosphere in the streets of Thimpu. I could feel the tension in the air. Many young men were roaming the streets, and I understood now how nightlife in Thimphu could get dangerous and become violent. I was glad to arrive safely in my hotel room.

I remembered that when I was in Thimphu for the first time in 1990, the biggest danger in the streets at night were the feral dogs, they often had rabies and always hunted in packs. We were told always to take stones with us or a stick, just in case the dogs attacked us. Now there are much more dangerous beings than dogs wandering the streets of Timphu. I felt sad. There are new types of bars in Bhutan, too. They also call themselves karaoke bars, but in those bars there are young girls whom you can pay to sing for you. This is the official story but I think there is much more going on there than singing.

Back at work on the hotel school, Karma the big hotel neighbour called on us. He had bought a whole Yak and he didn't know how to butcher it. Could we help?

"This is your chance", I told the boys, "why don't you do it?"

"I've never butchered a Yak", said Anton.

"Let's watch a YouTube video", I told him. So we did.

We went to Jigme's hotel and I brought my laptop and, following the instruction video, Anton and Adam started to attack the Yak like two samurai warriors. The animal was huge and after a few hours, the entire carcass was neatly divided into steaks, filets, meat for mincemeat for hamburgers, and many more.

"In the West they would never let you touch this valuable meat if you don't have a lot of experience being a butcher, this was a unique chance," Anton said.

"Sometimes you have to bluff to get ahead," I said, "and in the end we know much more about how to handle meat than the Bhutanese." We celebrated the work by eating a delicious Yak steak at Jigme's restaurant.

My time to go back home approached but Anton and Adam had it all under control, or so it seemed. I planned to come back half a year later when the renovation of the hotel, kitchen and the dorm was ready and the school would be up and running.

CHAPTER 20

THE LONELINESS OF
THE FUNDRAISER

Back in Amsterdam I continued fundraising. It was still going really well. My only problem was that I didn't earn a penny myself, because I put all the money towards the school and its success. Looking back this was a huge mistake. I should have budgeted a salary for myself, because I was not in a position to work for free. But I thought that, as the founder of a non-profit foundation, it wouldn't look good to include my own salary when I took the budget to potential donors.

Now I think that was wrong. I should have been paid for all my hard work. But we were operating from a state of scarcity. I thought all the money was needed for the school and to pay the experts. Without realising it, I had put myself in a position that I did not like at all! I hated fundraising and most of my time was spent doing work that I neither liked nor was paid for. My dream was to be actively involved with the school but instead I was chasing paperwork and donations.

It felt to me as if everybody benefitted except me. I also found working with Paolo increasingly difficult because of the distant. I was very grateful for all his support, financially and in other ways. Without his help the project would have take much longer to get it off the ground. But, I realised that I had inadvertently positioned myself in an unacceptable situation. I had to change this.

All the quotes about following your heart, being a pioneer, helping others instead of yourself, are very aspirational, but it's not that simple. We should have structured the school much better from the start. We should have planned and discussed how to run it and clarified the positions and responsibilities. Of course it was also very difficult to run the project while we were living in different countries. There was an overall lack of communication.

While Adam and Anton supervised the setup of the school in Bhutan, we had a lot of Skype meetings, and there were a lot of challenges. First of all, the visas for the boys were a huge issue. The immigration authorities of Bhutan refused to give the boys a 12 month work visa. Mr. Jigme had done his utmost to arrange the visas for them but to no effect. The immigration officer in Bhutan has all the power to do as he or she pleases. The man we had to deal with was known to be very difficult, he just didn't like to let people in, especially Westerners. Even Bhutanese professionals complained about this. Experts who were needed from outside could not come to Bhutan.

The only way was to buy a tourist visa and pay $250 per day.

"I need to go to the prime minister because this is crazy", Mr Jigme said. Anton and Adam needed to renew their Bhutanese visa, so they had to travel to India to wait there. They decided to go to Jagaon, the Indian border town. While they were waiting for their visas to clear, they could organise all the purchases for the hotel and school.

In the end, Anton and Adam had to wait almost three months in Jagoan. It's not the nicest place on the planet but the boys made the best of it. Finally they got their visas for a year's stay from the prime minister of Bhutan.

Now the school was set up, and I went to spend several weeks there. We started with 35 students and seven staff members. We hired the teachers from the five star hotels that already existed in Bhutan. So the housekeeper, food and beverage manager, front office manager and the chefs came from these hotels. They were very good teachers. The boys had done a very good job setting it all up.

Paolo came to join me for a short week, and we

had fun at the school. We went shopping to buy things to make the hotel rooms and restaurant cosier. It was such fun to be with the students, they were so eager to learn and so happy to be given a chance for a better future.

I'm a passionate cook, and I wanted to give some cooking lessons to the students, too. So I taught them how to make sushi. They loved it.

Through a friend I was connected with an American film maker who was living in Bhutan. She contacted me and wanted to visit me at the school. I said, "yes, why not." I told her that she needed to pay if she wanted to stay one night and eat in the restaurant.

On a Friday afternoon Anna came in her car, a typical new age Californian woman. Talking a lot, actually non-stop, and totally in awe of Bhutanese culture. However, she made a huge mistake, she confused the history of Thailand with the history of Bhutan! She was in her 40s, good looking and probably a party animal. She told me she needed a lot of love, so she really preferred to take younger lovers. She was used to this in the US, and she was not willing to change her lifestyle in Bhutan.

"This is a small country and there is a lot of gossip," I told her, "how can you sleep around with young guys? A woman of your age? This is going to look really bad."

"I'm a girl from America", she said, "and I'm not giving up my American lifestyle."

"But you are in Bhutan," I said, "this is a different culture and a very small country, you can't do this."

"I don't care", she said, "they should accept me as the person I am, and I'm not willing to adapt to them." I decided to change the subject.

"How on earth did you get your visa to be able to stay in Bhutan?"

"Oh," she said, "I'm friends with the king, so I can stay here as long as I like. The king has asked me to set up a film industry here in Bhutan."

I was very surprised.

"Yes, a film industry, I'm a film producer, and I'd like to do it, only I don't have money, I need to find an investor."

Paolo and I had some errands to do, and Anna said she would leave soon.

As we were driving back to our school, Paolo told

me: "I bet this Anna is still in the school." "Do you think so?" I said.

"Yes, I bet."

"Why would she?" I said.

"I don't know," said Paolo, "I just have a feeling."

We drove up to the school and yes, I could see her sitting in the bar, she had ordered a bottle of wine (it was 4 PM). She had almost finished the whole bottle of wine.

"Oh you are still here?" I asked.

"Yes, I thought I would stay the night."

We had all been invited for dinner at Mr Jigme's house. Of course he generously invited Anna to come along. Another Western woman who calls herself a Buddhist and who thinks Bhutan is Shangri La, I thought, just like the cellist and all the others.

We had a nice dinner at Mr. Jigme's house and after dinner I went home to go to bed. Paolo, Anton, Adam and Anna went out for a drink. Next morning Paolo and I had breakfast. Paolo told me that Anna had tried to seduce him last night. What!

"Yes", Paolo said, "it was very clear. She did all the

tricks to get me into her bed, but I just acted as if I didn't get it."

Later Mr. Jigme told me that she also tried to seduce his nephew. She asked for his phone number and if he wanted to take her out. The nephew was still very young and found her behaviour somewhat puzzling.

In the morning, Paolo and I had to go out. I wanted to give Anna the bill for the wine, hotel stay and breakfast but she was still sleeping, alone, as far as I know.

Later I heard from Adam that she had tried to sneak out without paying, but Adam stood in front of her car and demanded that she pay her bill. She started to argue that she had no money and that she thought she was my guest. Adam asked her to open her purse. All she had was a 1000 Ngultrum bill. He took it and asked her to pay the rest when she came back. Of course she never did!

CHAPTER 21

SPIRITS AT THE SCHOOL

There is never a dull moment in a hotel school.

The next night I woke up around 3 AM. There was a lot of noise in the hotel. The student dorm was on the third floor, and I could hear people walking in and out. I decided to get out of bed to take a look.

I walked upstairs into the girls' dorm where the commotion was coming from. All the girls were in a state of turmoil. Radikha the housekeeping teacher was also the dorm supervisor. She approached me and pointed to a skinny girl lying on the floor with four other girls holding her down. The girl was Sastika, a shy 17-year old. Her eyes were open and very dark, and her voice was strange. It was a deep dark voice that was incompatible with a girl of 17.

The voice was saying: "It's so nice to be here with all you girls, you all have beautiful long hair, I also want to have beautiful long hair." Then Sastika started to shake again violently. The girls had to hold her down very firmly.

"Sastika is possessed by a spirit," Radhika said, "she comes from a family that has a lot of mediums. We called her uncle to come and chase away the spirit that possessed her." A few minutes later, an older man in a Nepalese outfit came in with a drum and started a ritual. I went back to my room and tried to get some more sleep. The next day I saw Sastika and asked her how she felt. She said that she had eaten beef the previous night and it was a full moon. This always happened to her when she ate beef under a full moon. Sastika is a Hindu with Nepali heritage. To eat beef is a sin for Hindus, but she said she liked it so much she couldn't resist. Later I heard that Sastika went home to be trained as a medium. She did not finish the hotel school.

The following days came and went with no major incidents. I gave cooking and baking lessons and explained to the kids about different foods in the world. One evening I had dinner with five female students from the food and beverage department.

This was our practice. Three male students had to serve us, while the girls needed to assess the waiters. This was a big thing for the girls. They dressed up as if they were going to a fancy restaurant. They were giggling and at 8 PM we sat down at a beautifully set table, the work of yet another group of students.

One cute girl asked me: "Madam, for what use is this?" She showed me the napkin. I had to laugh, of course in Bhutan people don't use napkins, they eat with their hands and after dinner they wash their hands with a few kernels of rice, or now, in more modern times, with water.

Then I saw another girl put the bread on her plate and eat it with a knife and fork. I explained that this was not the way to eat bread! The girls were so eager to learn. One said to me: "Oh, madam, I'm so proud to be here at this school. Here I learn how to behave in fancy places and when a boy takes me out, I know all the right things to do." I said: "Yes, now you have become a woman of the world!" I just love all these kids.

Two days later Adam came to me and told me that a whole bottle of cognac was empty. I had brought this bottle to stock the bar because European spirits are very expensive in Bhutan.

"Do you know if someone was very drunk recently?" I said. "No", Adam replied, "I'll find out."

In a place where 50 kids live together day and night it's very hard to keep secrets and a few hours later Adam found the culprit. A young guy, who wanted to taste the liquor, liked it so much that he and his friend finished the whole bottle. He was very sick afterwards. Adam warned him that he had to pay back the price of the bottle and if this happened again he would be expelled from the school. In the end he became a good student and graduated with honours.

YOUNG PEOPLE OF BHUTAN

I know where these kids come from. I lived in a village in Bhutan myself and most of these children come from villages just like Tsachaphu. They often have illiterate parents. They are the first or second generation in their village that had access to education at high school level. Given these circumstances their parents want them to find a good job, so they can earn a good salary. But there are not many jobs for them. They don't want to stay in the village but have no idea how to improve themselves or get more education, and of course their parents often can't afford it. They also have no guidance or information about the opportunities that are open to them. Another group of young people in a very difficult position are of Nepalese descent. They are regarded as non-Bhutanese, although their families have often lived in Bhutan for generations. As non-Bhutanese citizens, they don't receive an ID card from the government and without which you have no access to state sponsored schools or institutions. They can't even get a mobile phone! Many of them have pleaded with the king of Bhutan for recognition but the king keeps ignoring their plight.

What we observed was that, in general, all these kids lacked the life skills needed to function in a modern world. I noticed that even with a high school diploma, they hardly knew anything about the world. Their education was mainly geared towards Bhutan and the history of Bhutan, which is very mythological. They've never been taught any facts about politics, colonialism, or democracy. But a real eye-opener for me was that they didn't know how to do something as simple as planning a day. Of course I remembered very vividly that linear time, as we know it in the West, didn't exist in the village. It was impossible to ask anybody when or on which day something would happen. Now, these high school graduates were still operating on the same concept of village time. If you told them they had to start their new job on Monday at 9 AM, they would not show up.

For example, we arranged internships for them in a five star hotel in the capital. Four of our students had to start on a Monday morning at 9 AM. But the hotel management called us to say that the four students had not reported for work. We could not believe it. One of the teachers called the kids and learned they were just at home relaxing. The teacher asked him, "why are you at home? You were supposed to start your internship at 9 AM this morning!" He replied, "oh, sir, I just forgot. I will come tomorrow."

This time issue happened all the time. I helped Thinley, a young Bhutanese girl, who was the best student from the second batch to a three month internship in Amsterdam at a four star hotel. She stayed with me in my house. She loved being in Amsterdam and didn't want to go home again. I wondered if I had perhaps made a huge mistake by giving her the chance to be in Europe for three months. She got a taste of freedom, friendship and some money. She went out with her colleagues to bars and coffee shops and she had such a good time. She told me that in her village in Bhutan, people would gossip if she went out with friends. And of course there was nothing she could go to. Paro only has a few seedy clubs where you can pay a girl to dance for you. This is not a nice environment for young girls to enjoy themselves. She saw that if you are willing to work, you can make a good life in the

West. She didn't want to go back, and she asked me to help her to get a job in Europe, but it is very hard to get a work permit for someone from South Asia.

But even she developed a different concept of time. Her shift started at 11 AM but she went to work at 8 AM.

I asked her, "Thinley, where are you going so early?"

"To work, madam."

"What time do you need to start?"

"At 11 AM!"

"Why are you going now?"

She looked at me with a blank face and could not answer. I showed her how to use a diary, where she could note all her working hours, then look at it every day so she knew what time to start.

The new age people are always talking about living in the moment. In Bhutan they live in the moment! But in modern times when you want to get things done, living in the moment can be a challenge.

One day, back at the school, I needed to go to Timphu and had to take a taxi. I was standing in Bongde, a small dusty town just a few kilometres from Thimphu. The town has several shops, a butcher, several groceries, and some bars. In the middle of the town there was a small roundabout and many stray dogs were lying in the sun. They were all sleeping, exhausted from a long night of barking. Everybody who has been to Bhutan knows the night barking of the packs of stray dogs that keep you up all night. In Thimphu it is so bad that every hotel has its own pack, so changing hotels doesn't help much to get a quiet night's sleep. Cows were also roaming the street and sadly enough they were eating the plastic from the garbage people threw into the river and onto the riverside. Most of the houses were red from beetle nut spit. So Bongde is not the most charming place in Bhutan. In the middle of town there is a taxi stand, where I waited for a taxi. A few minutes later a small green car approached me and I got in. The driver just looked just like the prime minister of Bhutan. I had to laugh when I mentioned the resemblance to him.

"Yes," he said, "I know I look just like him."

He told me his name was Nidup. He asked me if I had been to Bhutan before, and I told him my stories, also about Tsachaphu.

"I am from Tsachaphu", he said. "I was very small when you stayed in my village. My house is in Tonfugin next to Phub Dorji's house"

"Aaah!" I said, "how wonderful to meet you."

Nidub told me he was now a taxi driver in Paro, and he was married with a daughter. I looked at him and realised how handsome he was. He had a dark brown very smooth face and friendly eyes.

"I go back regularly to Tsachaphu," he said, "there is now an unpaved road all the way to the village, and some households have cars now."

"What! Cars in Tsachaphu!" Somehow I couldn't believe it.

"Yes", Nidup said, "I tried to help the people there to improve the road but it is so hard. One rainy season and everything is mud again."

He drove in silence for a while. I was still trying to imagine a road to Tsachaphu and the villagers driving around in cars.

"You stayed with Aum Zam, right?" Nidup said. "Yes!" I said.

"She passed away a few years ago," he continued, "and Panghe, her son, now lives in her house."

Aum Zam dead! I felt that a whole way of life had disappeared. It only lived in memory now.

"Because Tsachaphu is so remote," Nidup said, "it is hard to improve the village. They have electricity now and latrines, but the village lacks people because most of the young people leave the village and leave the old people behind."

"That's sad", I said.

"Some go back to help their families grow rice and do other agricultural work," said Nidup. "I'm going to Tsachaphu next month, why don't you come with me."

"I would love to come," I said, "but I won't be in Bhutan."

"Ok, then we do it next time."

"I would love to," I said.

Then Nidup asked me something strange: "Did you adopt a Bhutanese child?"

"No!" I said, "why would I do that?"

"You are all rich, you could pay for a Bhutanese child to go to school and many other things," he said, "a lot of *chillips* do that."

"I've helped a lot of Bhutanese the last 26 years," I said, "and my current project is the Bongde School for Tourism and Hospitality, a major project with a lot of money invested."

"Oh," he said, "that is good then."

We reached Thimpu and exchanged phone numbers. Sadly I have not seen him again since, and I never had a chance to go back to the village.

We had built a pizza oven outside the hotel. Every last Saturday of the month, the staff organised a pizza party, and many foreigners and locals came to join us. The most loyal guests were the foreign workers from the other five star hotels in Paro and of course there was always a large group of Drukair pilots, most of them Greek.

Because it was my last evening at the school, the students put on a show, especially for me. It was so sweet.

They had made a bonfire in the patio of the hotel school, right next to the pizza oven. They had arranged chairs around the fire and there was a sound system so we could dance.

All the students gathered, and they started to dance for me. It felt so warm and kind. They had even collected money to buy me a gift. I could have hugged them all. This is why it is great to do something for other people, I loved seeing how much the students appreciated me. The evening was fun. We all danced together and I danced the sirtaki with one of the Greek pilots. I asked him how he had ended up in Bhutan. He told me that he lost his job when Olympic Airways, the Greek national airline, went bankrupt many years ago. He couldn't get work in Europe, and Asia was much better. Then he heard that Bhutan needed pilots but they needed to have extra training for the difficult airport of Paro. I had heard this many times and had in fact experienced it once myself. We couldn't land in Paro because of a strong wind and had to fly back to Kolkata in India to spend the night there and wait for better weather.

But to him, that seemed very attractive, so he and the three other Greek pilots decided to do the training and moved to Bhutan.

So after an evening of great fun with all those warm-hearted, lovely students, I went to bed very happy.

The next day, flying out of Bhutan to Bangkok, the pilot from the night before was flying my plane. About half an hour into the flight, he invited me come and to sit with him in the cockpit.

I sat and looked into the sky as we were flying out of the mountains into the air. The weather was clear, I could see the wide plains of India with its big rivers shining like silver ribbons.

I didn't know then that this would be my last flight out of Bhutan.

CHAPTER 22

DIFFICULT RELATIONSHIPS

Now I am sitting at my desk in Amsterdam writing this book. As I look at a grey Dutch sky outside, I imagine the crisp mountains of Bhutan against the blue sky and the very bright yellow sunlight. In my mind the colours of Bhutan are blue, maroon, yellow and orange.

My mind is full of memories. But strangely I don't miss the country. At some point I realised it was a blessing in disguise to be blacklisted, because it forced me to reflect on my relationship with Bhutan and all the work that I did for that place. I realise that I became too involved. I gave it too much and it took too much from me.

It was like being in an unhealthy marriage.

For most of the time during the hotel school project, I was not happy. I wanted to be much more directly involved, teaching and running it, but it was impossible, partly because I had to do fundraising in Europe, and partly because of the arbitrary visa regulations. The head of immigration didn't like what we were doing or he did not like Mr Jigme, and most of our visa requests were rejected. We had to fight all the time to send a teacher to our school. So much power in the hand of just one man! But that was Bhutan. A side of Bhutan I didn't want to see before.

I thought that by studying the culture, history and religion of a country you get to know it. And it's true that you learn a lot about the country that way, but you don't learn about the mentality of its people. I realised that by becoming an entrepreneur, I had learned so much more about the people of Bhutan. I learned things you just can't learn as an academic.

As for the project, my initial plan was to do an impact investment project. Of course, when I got the idea I didn't know that my plan was called an impact project. Impact investment is a relatively new concept but actually it is very old. Before it was called "impact investing" it was called sustainable investment. It basically means that you invest in a company or project that has a good return on investment, creates jobs for local people, and respects the environment. Many traditional investors, especially Americans, confuse this with philanthropy, but it isn't. It's mainstream investing but with ethics. It excludes, however, investments in weapons, harmful chemicals and other things that are destructive for humans and the planet.

When I first got the idea of creating a culturally authentic for-profit high-end eco-lodge hotel in Bumthang, it made sense to me to also create a hotel school as a non-profit project alongside it. I knew that most kids, to whom I wanted to give a chance, wouldn't have the money to pay school fees.

Because impact investing was still a very new concept around 2010, it was hard to get investment money for the five star eco-lodge. It was far easier to get donations for the school. Paolo and I invested a lot in setting up a proper business, creating a fully-fledged business plan and a financial model. We also built a professional team with a good track record. Despite these factors I never managed to get enough investment money to build the hotel. So we focused on the school.

I learned that it is far easier for wealthy people to

give donation to an established foundation than to invest in a for-profit project. These donations are tax deductible and easy to manage. To invest is costly because they have to do due diligence and start up investment in frontier markets is very risky. I also learned that a small amount of investment money (any amount under $10 million) is not interesting for investors, the due diligence and management of a small sum is too expensive for a profitable return on their investment.

During the fundraising in support of the for-profit eco-lodge, I also learned that many of the organisations who claim to help impact entrepreneurs in emerging markets are not doing what they say they do. I went to most of them and found that they don't help start-ups in frontier markets. Like the private investors, they consider it too risky. The only thing a start-up entrepreneur can do is find an angel investor who knows the country and is willing to take a risk. The investment companies mostly invest in entities that are already established and are making a profit. So it's very demanding work, and the only way to succeed is by never giving up. Of course, it's also a good way to fail.

My project in Bhutan was not only altruistic. I had hoped to generate a decent income for myself from the for-profit hotel. I was hoping that the school could later be financed through a portion of the hotel's profit. But because of lack of investment, we set up the school in Bongde as a hybrid model, partly as a for-profit hotel and restaurant and partly as a school, with student dorms attached and the conference room divided into classrooms. The students train working with real hotel guests and half their time is spent in classroom education.

Interestingly, many professionals from the hospitality and tourism industry found my idea of combining the for-profit hotel with the non-profit school brilliant. But it still didn't work. I learned from this project that the hospitality sector is a difficult one to do things your way. In Bhutan and often in emerging markets it's very hard to get investments if you are not part of a big hotel chain, these chains have their own in-house training and they can spread the risk because they have so many hotels in different parts of a country and indeed in many different countries. And then there are also the family-run hotels who are often not very well managed. But it is these small family run hotels that create the most jobs for the community, and the money they make mostly stays in the country.

The good thing about Bhutan was that the country had a clean slate. My vision was to start a whole new way of presenting culturally-authentic hospitality, and to include ancient Bhutanese etiquette into the hospitality. Tourists are visiting Bhutan for a unique experience and we could give them a glimpse of that exquisite heritage and preserve it at the same time. I wanted to use only Bhutanese fabrics and woodwork in the hotel and also present Bhutanese cuisine in a refined and authentic way. Bhutanese cuisine is not very complex, it's very much farm food. It is not as developed as the Indian or Thai royal culinary arts but the produce Bhutan has is of very good quality and much can be done to create more and interesting dishes.

THE POWER OF MONEY: HIGH PRICE, HIGH VALUE

My life as an academic was one of blissful ignorance of the ways of the world. I believed in the goodness of people. Six years struggling to get the school off the ground showed me the 'real' world. The world of money and power.

At some point it got too much for me, and for two years I was very depressed. I could no longer cope with the lies, the cheating, and the narcissism that I encountered everywhere.

I became also very disappointed in the Bhutanese people whom I knew and helped so much. I was shocked to learn that many of the people I had known for many year, and brought a lot of business to, were not very interested in helping us with the hotel school. I asked the travel agencies I had worked with for decades to bring their customers to us because this would help us a lot and didn't cost them anything, but they didn't care! I learned that compassion can be a very empty sentiment. For many of my Bhutanese friends, compassion didn't mean actively helping someone. During my depression I lost my connection with them because they didn't understand what I was going through. Some of them judged me and misjudged me. I felt very lonely.

The worst thing about being depressed is that it feels endless. You are in a black hole and nothing interests you or makes you happy. Everybody and everything is dark. For years I had been so hopeful but again and again I had to cope with disappointments. If you try to bring a project to life as I had done, you have to give more than 100% of yourself. My husband understood that and he supported me fully. But it took so long and along the way we had to cope with a financial crisis that had a big impact on our private lives. I couldn't afford to work for free anymore, so I tried to find paying jobs. But in the current job market, if you are over 50, nobody will hire you. It was a very tough time.

Once in a while I would meet a person who understood what I'd done, and it was sheer bliss to connect with someone who related to my journey, with all its joys and pain.

Ironically, my depression started to heal after I learned that I was blacklisted because this huge burden was taken from my shoulders. Now I was free again! I could move on. I wish I knew who blacklisted me in Bhutan - I would like to send this person a thank you note. Through the grapevine I heard that it might be someone from the royal family. I am not surprised.

FREEDOM FROM THE BLACK LIST

Writing this book feels so liberating. It is wonderful to be free and tell my story. Before I always had to be careful and politically correct because I was afraid of the consequences. Even famous people have been blacklisted because they wrote something the royals did not like. One such person was Michael Aris, the late husband of Aung San Suu Kyi. Michael wrote a book about *Pema Lingpa*, one of the saints of Bhutan. It's a scholarly book, I can't see any controversial issues in it, but I am not Bhutanese. Unni Wikan, a much respected anthropologist from Norway, published the tragic life story of a Bhutanese nun. The author got blacklisted.

Now that I am blacklisted too, I am free to tell my story.

The Bhutanese have never told me the reason for my being blacklisted. I wrote to the embassies in Brussels and Bangkok. Brussels never replied and Bangkok told me that Mr Jigme, who was my counterpart, had to solve my problem. But Mr Jigme was always sent away from the immigration office. They told him that they couldn't tell him anything because of national security. This was strange because I am not a spy, nor do I work in politics. I am not a threat to society, or wait a minute, maybe I am?

After approaching embassies to no avail, I wrote a letter to his majesty the King. Of course I never received a reply. Then one day I met a gentleman with a lot of power and influence. He loved the work I had done in Bhutan. This gentleman was a guest at the Amsterdam hotel where Thinley, a Bhutanese student from my hotel school, worked as an intern. He was very impressed with her professionalism and asked her where she came from. She told him that she was from Bhutan.

"From Bhutan!" the gentleman said, "where did you learn your skills?"

"At the hotel school in Bhutan," she said.

"There is a good hotel school in Bhutan?" the man asked.

"Yes," Thinley said, "it was set up by a Dutch lady, and I live with her here in Amsterdam for three months."

The gentleman wanted to meet me!

So, soon afterwards, we met. I told him my story. He was not surprised that I was on the blacklist. He knew Asia very well and Bhutan, particularly well. He told me that Bhutan is a very difficult country to do anything in, especially with investments. You can never be sure that you will get your money out of the country again, and even much worse things (that you would never think of) can happen. So this gentlemen said he would try to find out for me why I had been blacklisted. And indeed, he later called me to let me know that I had supposedly insulted a member of the royal family on Facebook.

I had many young Bhutanese friends on Facebook and there were often discussions. But I can honestly say that I have never insulted any Bhutanese citizen, as far as I know, but that's just it. I don't know.

I live and grew up in the West, where we have

freedom of speech. In Bhutan there is no freedom of speech, journalists cannot do their work, they are not allowed to report on corruption or other shady practices, and certainly nothing that involves members of the royal family. I learned that the royals in Bhutan can do anything they want and get away with it. One friend of mine told me that he was in Bhutan and went to a club where he saw a girl he wanted to dance with. Many other guys told him to stay away from her because a prince wanted to dance with her too.

My friend, a typical Westerner, said, "if the girl doesn't want to dance with me, she can say so!" The guys told him he would be beaten up if he didn't stay away from the girl, princes have all the power.

When I did the leadership programme in Bumthang with the 50 unemployed young people, a Bhutanese friend told me to stay away as far as possible from the royal family because if they want you to work for them, this means you have to work for free, you will never get paid! And you lose all your freedom and have to dance to their tune. I didn't want that, so I never reached out to the royals.

All Bhutanese worship the fourth King, he did

so much good in Bhutan. Many Bhutanese say that the fourth King is a God to them, but he made one mistake and that was to marry the four sisters who became the four queens of Bhutan. These four queens are very skilled at taking good care of themselves and now the fifth king is still young and doesn't have the wisdom of his father.

I realised living in the West and doing a project in a country like Bhutan is not easy. We are so used to our freedom. We have equality, we have laws that protect us, and there is a certain level of transparency.

Considering that none of this exists in Bhutan, it is ironic that the Western world admires the country so much for its Gross National Happiness. The Bhutanese are very good at propaganda for GNH. Having said that, many Bhutanese themselves call it the Gross National Hypocrites because the people, who work for the Centre of Bhutan studies, this institution is responsible to implement the GNH principles into Bhutanese society are the unhappiest people in Bhutan. They once stayed at the hotel school for a week. I found out that they were not happy at all but very arrogant, and had a total lack of social skills.

We in the West are naïve to believe that one of the poorest countries in the world, which has no freedom of speech, no protection of human rights, and where people don't have the right to protest or demonstrate is one of the happiest places in the world. We wouldn't be happy if our rights were taken away.

And then there is the treatment of minorities in Bhutan. People who are descendants of the Nepalese migrants who came to live in Bhutan several generation ago are excluded from society and don't have citizenship. Their rights are restricted and so are their lives.

There was a time when I also looked at Bhutan through rose-coloured glasses. To me, the world in Bhutan looked so peaceful. I immersed myself in the holistic way of life, which felt like such a warm bath after all the stress from living in industrialised countries with all their environmental problems. Bhutan was still whole, and nature was still magnificent. The Bhutanese people had a wonderful relationship with nature, and there was a lot to learn from them for the rest of the world. But I'm afraid that, in only 20 years, the country accelerated like a rocket from a medieval culture with a barter economy into the complex global twenty-first century economy. It all happened far too fast. The international development organisations loved Bhutan and much money has been poured into the country. Bhutan had a well-functioning government and because of this it became the favourite child of these agencies. Many famous people visited Bhutan and they all gave a lot of money. Many Western Buddhists donated to, sponsored, supported, adopted and promoted the country. So Bhutan became spoiled. We cannot hold that against them but it corrupted the people a lot. Nowadays it's the rich Buddhists from Hong Kong and Taiwan who come to Bhutan to visit a lama and pay handsomely for his services. A new temple has been built in the last few years right next to our hotel school. It was commissioned and paid for by a rich Chinese man from Hong Kong after he was cured by a Bhutanese lama. Everywhere in Bhutan you can see new temples being built. It is sad because the ancient temples with marvellous wall paintings from the fifteenth century are neglected.

CHAPTER 23

A SWEATSHOP ON PARK AVENUE

N ot all the chapters of my love story with Bhutan and my life between two cultures, East and West, happened in Bhutan itself. One of the most outrageous episodes took place in New York, the epitome of Western modernity. I am including it here because it is a perfect example of a situation in which the misunderstandings and cultural exploitation happen in the name of exotic spirituality, allowing Westerners to use people from developing countries for monetary gain and fame.

In the summer of 2015 I received a call from someone from New York, who told me that I had been spotted because of my Ph.D. book on Bhutan. At first I was a bit sceptical but after a long conversation it became clear that he was working for Taryn Simon, an American multidisciplinary artist, whom I had never heard of. Conner, her assistant, explained to me that Simon was planning a new big work of art in an armoury in New York, a famous avant-garde gallery. It was going to be a big live performance with funeral and death rituals from all over the world. They asked me if I was willing to help them with information about death rituals in Bhutan.

Of course I could help! And I loved what I heard. I'd often thought that we need to preserve our death rituals. A year before, when the uncle of a friend from the US died, I asked if there would be a funeral.

"No", he said, "we won't have a funeral, we will just have him cremated and announce his death on Facebook."

What a poor way to honour a life! I was a bit shocked when I heard that. Death rituals are beautiful rituals in all religions, honouring the soul of the departed, bringing people together and celebrating the life and passing of the loved one. In many cultures, death rituals are the most elaborate ones in human life and often the most expensive and important as well.

I remembered the Bhutanese village where even the poorest paid into a funeral insurance every week.

To bring many cultures together and show the world how rich we are in these rituals would be wonderful. So I told Conner I was very happy to help. We had many Skype conversations and I had one conversation with Simon herself. I had to write down the *bardo* rituals and explain to them what it was all about. The project required many hours of work.

Half a year later Conner asked me if I could find three Bhutanese monks to come to the armoury in New York for three weeks to show their rituals. He told me I could be there with them and all of us would be paid. I thought the US was a civilised country, and so I assumed they would treat us with respect and pay us fairly.

In November 2015 when I was in Bhutan working on the hotel school I asked a friend if he knew three monks who would be willing to go to the US. Of course every monk would be very glad to get a chance like that. This friend told me not to worry and he would find me three 'clean' monks, as he put it. In Bhutan, 'clean' monks means monks who live like real monks. Not monks who do all the things monks shouldn't do, like having girlfriends, drinking alcohol and many other things.

When I was back in Netherlands, Conner asked me a lot of questions that I had to ask the monks. The Bhutanese friend I communicated with was very bad at answering the questions and 'his' monks where never available. Many monks do live in remote villages or are not in contact with the world, meditating on a mountain.

In March 2016 I returned to Bhutan and told my friend that I wanted to meet at least one of the monks because we urgently needed to deal with a lot of paperwork, and I needed to answer all the questions Conner had. I also asked Conner if they could pay me for my time. I had put in so many hours and had given them my knowledge. He told me they had no budget to pay the anthropologists who made this project possible, but they would invite us to come to New York and we would get paid for our time there. It was not much, but I still believed in the project and thought that they would acknowledge all the anthropologists who worked for them.

Back in Bhutan and the hotel school, I met my friend and the senior monk that he thought would be good for the project in New York. The monk immediately requested that the kitchen cook him some food. He also demanded tea and cookies. His first question was if I would give him money so that he could buy all kinds of things for his New York trip. I didn't like him at all. I really didn't want to spend three weeks in New York with this guy. He ate his food, of course without paying, and he left after telling me again how much money he wanted. I called my friend and told him that I didn't wanted to go to the US with this monk. After a heated debate I kept to my decision and cancelled the collaboration. Now I had nothing!

The next day I met Wangdi, a friend of a friend. I told him my problem and he said: "I can help you, the Lam Neten of Paro is a good friend of mine and he would love to be part of such a project, he also has good lamas that can go with him." A Lam Neten is the head monk of a *dzong*, or big monastery. His status is comparable with a cardinal in the Catholic Church. The very same day, Wangdi organised an audience with the Lam Neten in his private quarters in the *dzong* of Paro, a gigantic fortress from the seventeenth century with hundreds of monks. It was very impressive to enter the main gate. These huge monasteries go back to the time before 1917 when Bhutan was a theocracy, just like Tibet. There is usually also a 'city hall' or administrative unit in the compound.

In the middle of the *dzong* is a courtyard, surrounded by and all the buildings. It has a distinctive feel of the middle ages. I had to follow a monk who guided me through the dark narrow corridors and up some very steep stairs to the private quarters of the Lam.

I was surprised to see a very friendly man with a wonderful smile looking at me. He didn't speak English and his niece, a beautiful young lady in full traditional Bhutanese costume, told me she was there to translate. Lam Neten was sitting in the lotus position on a pillow in front of a huge altar full of Buddha statues and *thangkhas*. I was sitting on a traditional Bhutanese bench with handcrafted tables in front of me, typical for the Tibetan world. As soon as I sat down, a young monk came up to me and offered me tea and biscuits. Lam Neten radiated peace and an amazing, calming energy. I could see that this was an accomplished spiritual person.

Lam asked me what the project was about. I explained everything to him as I knew it at the time, and he was very happy to tell me that he would like to participate. He also could take two of his monks with him. One of them was Sonam who had been to the West several times and spoke good English. I was happy to hear this because my Dzongkha was not good enough to do full translations. I explained to Lam that we needed to fill in all the forms for the US visa. This was a real pain in the neck and needed a lot of attention to details. All three of them also would need to go to the USA embassy in Delhi in India to apply for their visas in person. The two other monks were just as kind as Lam and I was happy with them. A few days after I had met Lam Neten and his friends Sonam and Phurba who would come with me to the US, I went home with a good feeling.

While we were waiting for the visa approval, I needed to work quite a bit on Taryn Simon's project. I still didn't know exactly what to expect. The only thing

I knew was that the lamas would have to perform their rituals for 20 minutes and then have a break. I thought that would not be so bad, since they were used to long days of performing rituals.

In Amsterdam I was waiting for the visa approval. The armoury had put all the papers for the visas together, even lawyers were involved to make sure the lamas could come to the US. But then I received an email from Sonam that he and Phurba got their visas but Lam Neten was rejected. I could not believe it. A man of that standing! He would never stay illegally in the US. Now, looking back on it, I think that it was a blessing in disguise. I would have been so embarrassed had he come to the armoury and been subjected to the kind of treatment that was in store for us. So now I had only two monks but it didn't seem to be a problem.

In September 2016 I flew from Amsterdam to New York and the lamas came from Bhutan. We had to report to the Sheraton Hotel in Hoboken, New Jersey, where we had rooms for three weeks. All performers arrived on the same day. There were three people from Greece, one lady from Ghana, one man from Ecuador, two ladies from Venezuela, one lady from Borneo, four men from Burkina Faso, four Yazidi's from France, three ladies from Dagestan, three ladies from Azerbaijan, one from Romania, one from Albania, three from South India, four men from Cambodia, three ladies from Kyrgyzstan, and one lady from Romania. All the performers were accompanied by anthropologists who could translate, because most of them came from very remote villages and didn't speak English. It was such a joy to meet all these people with their colourful dresses and costumes. It was such a rich display of people and cultures..

During our initial night in the hotel, we met Taryn Simon for the first time, a skinny woman in her late 30s with long blonde hair, wearing kind of silly designer dress that made her look like Dorothy in the Wizard of Oz. She greeted us and told us that she was so excited that we are all there. There had been many visa rejections, especially with the group from Ghana, only one lady could come instead of four. Taryn was very upset with the visa policies of the US. Yet, most of us had made it.

We were given some bad food in the hotel, tasteless salad with some dry sandwiches.

After Taryn's introduction we were all given the schedule for the coming weeks. Together with Marina, the Romanian anthropologist, I looked at the schedule.

"Is this legal?" Marina asked.

And she was right, it was an exploitative schedule. We had to work three weeks in a row, with only one day off. We then needed to start the next day at 11 AM and work until midnight. Long days were needed to rehearse the show and get it all in place. I told Marina, "in New York they have labour laws, they cannot do this to us." But in the end they did.

So the next day a bus came to pick us up to take us from the hotel to the Armoury on Park Avenue, the ritziest part of New York. Our colourful ethnic group looked so out of place in that street. In the Armoury we were guided backstage, having to wait till Taryn called us. In the main hall of the Armoury, a huge hall as big as a football field, the artist had erected eleven very high, narrow concrete towers. In these towers, each only a few square meters wide, with a small entrance, the performers had to sit and do their mourning rituals.

The anthropologists who had found the performers in all the countries and who had to translate for them were forced to spend all their time backstage. We were only needed when Taryn Simon wanted a translation or had any questions.

The three ladies from Azerbaijan were very religious Muslims, dressed in black from head to toe. All three carried a small black handbag that they had with them all the time, even when they walked to the breakfast buffet. The three ladies from Dagestan wore the typical clothes for older women in Central Asia: headscarves and skirts with a floral designs, blouses and woollen vests, and thick brown stockings. The lady from Ghana was dressed in colourful African attire and wore a cute little football around her neck. Later I found out that it was her mobile phone. She had the most beautiful smile. The gentleman from Ecuador was blind, he was a singer and accordion player. The lady from Albania was older and wore the traditional Albanian costume. Of course the lamas always wore maroon monk's ropes. The Yazidi and the

Greeks (two men and a woman) wore black clothes. The Cambodians wore traditional Cambodian clothes during the performance but Western clothes during the day.

The four men from Burkina Faso brought with them an amazing mask that was larger than a man and very heavy. It was a very sacred mask. The lady from Borneo was a *dayak* from a longhouse, a very sweet tiny person. She was mostly dressed in batique clothes from her homeland. The Indian women wore saris, always very beautiful.

At the rehearsals Taryn was working on creating the show according to her vision. All these performers brought sacred objects with them that they normally needed when they were performing the rituals at home. But Taryn thought that was not avant-garde enough, and she wanted to make it minimalistic, totally disregarding the deeper meaning of the rituals and the feelings of the performers. Many of the performers started to complain that they could not perform their rituals properly without their sacred objects in the towers. They said, we will offend the gods, and we cannot do that. Some told me that since Taryn wasn't taking them seriously they would just fake the rituals. They didn't want to offend their gods!

And they were right. The show didn't respect all the various religions whose practitioners they had gathered together. On the contrary, they were exhibited like exotic specimens in a zoo for the enjoyment of paying customers.

We were all so tired and the food was so bad, both breakfast at the hotel and dinner in the Armoury. I talked to the organiser and asked her if she could at least arrange for some rice (almost all the people were from rice-eating countries) and some spicy dishes. The rice came but no spicy dishes.

After a week of long days the opening day of the performance came closer. Taryn was happy with her show. In all eleven towers, religious practitioners from eleven different cultures had to perform their death rituals at the same time. The performance lasted 20 minutes and it was a cacophony of wailing, Cambodian gamelan, Bhutanese horns and drums, polyphonic singing from the Greeks, crying from the Ghanaian lady, singing and flutes from the Yazidi, singing and accordion playing from the blind player from Ecuador and banging on wood by the Romanian lady. The audience would come in for 20 minutes and during this time they could visit each of the towers, go inside and spend a few minutes with the mourners. It was a powerful experience, they said. Some visitors had to cry. Taryn told us that many famous people came to see the performance, for example: Salman Rushdie and several pop stars.

After the 'performance', there was a short break and then it started all over again until midnight.

Morale was good for the first ten days. But after that, people started to complain about the bad food, the long days, and overall sheer exhaustion. Interestingly, the Bhutanese lamas said nothing. The production crew told me that Taryn had spent millions on the concrete towers. To her they were a symbol of the towers of silence of the Parsi faith. Still, we received $20 pocket money per day, yet our working conditions were awful. The next day in the morning I called a very well-connected friend in Washington DC. He told me we should all get out. But most of the performers were from developing countries and they were waiting for the small pay-out at the end of our time in New York.

They wanted to save as much as they could to pay for their children's school fees or to repair their houses. It also seemed that everyone was afraid of Taryn. I wrote an email to Conner since he was my contact person. I told Conner what was going on backstage. We needed rest and better food.

Two days later, I was backstage and the Ghanaian lady was not feeling well. She was so exhausted and could not perform anymore. Taryn went to her and told her she had to go into the tower that it was important. Taryn reassured her that she would get her medicine, so she could perform again. I heard everything. All the production people backstage looked at each other but nobody dared to speak up. I thought I had nothing to lose, so I went to up her and told her: "Taryn, what are you doing? We are all human beings and the times when you could abuse people like this are over. I feel I am living in the times of Charles Dickens. Don't you have any scruples?"

She looked at me in shock, I think no one had ever talked to her like that.

"Why don't you complain to the board of the Armoury?" she said.

I told her I had written to Conner but she said she didn't believe me and refused to look at his inbox.

"I'm very happy to talk to the board of the Armoury," I said, "and tell them what is going on here. Maybe they don't care either, I don't know, but it is very easy to exploit these people."

"Why don't you leave", she said. I thought that would be an easy way out for her. I wasn't going to leave and leave my monks here alone.

I also want my small payment on the last day of our stay.

From that moment on I was excluded from the project. Later I heard that a young man was escorted out of the Armoury building by two policemen because he was the only one who told Taryn that he didn't want to work under these conditions. Taryn was so angry that she called the police to have him removed. The guy was a nice young man and far from being aggressive or violent. I saw more and more of the dark underbelly of the New York art world.

Many of us had given Taryn our knowledge for free. Marina, the Romanian anthropologist, told me that her name was mentioned nowhere in the exhibition materials. We had given the artist our intellectual property for free and we had become invisible.

I've seen a TED talk by Taryn Simon in which she claims to be a spokesperson for the downtrodden of this world. It's all a scam and lies. This woman is all about ego.

I stayed on, tried to make the best of it and made friends with the religious practitioners and some of the crew. Now I was so happy that the Lam Neten was not there, I would have been so embarrassed with the treatment he would have received.

In the end most of the 'mourners' faked their performances, they saw that there was no respect whatsoever for the transcendental values and sacredness of their rituals. It was only for show and for the New Yorkers who could afford to pay $40 to poorly paid people from the developing world, exhibited like exotic cultural specimens.

We did receive our payment on the final day. Everyone received an invitation to participate in a new project planned the next year in London. Except me of course, but I didn't want to have anything to do with this anymore. My lesson was that in time of distress I noticed only very few people speak up. Most keep their mouth shut because they are afraid to lose their work or pay- check.

I contacted many journalists in New York to ask them what I could do to tell the world about our experience on this project. One journalist from a famous art magazine told me that Taryn got away with breaking the labour laws because she claimed to have a performance with sculptures (the towers) but she conveniently forgot to mention that there were human beings in those towers. Another journalist was interested to write about this but he wanted to interview the performers. But most of them lived in remote villages and didn't speak English. Also they didn't know the ways of the West, it would be very difficult.

Personally, I couldn't understand how this Taryn Simon can live with herself, she is very well connected and wealthy; her husband is the brother of a famous Hollywood actress. It seems she lacks any form of compassion.

CHAPTER 24

CAN YOU REPEAT THIS? SUCCESS AND OTHER COUNTRIES

In 2015 we opened the doors of our school and when it became a success within a short period of time, other people asked me to set up similar projects in Kenya, in Myanmar and in the north of Thailand. In 2016 I was asked by a Thai organisation to set up a hotel and school in Karen State, Myanmar. They were the only company who ever paid me for this kind of work. I found investors and got a huge donations, but the project stopped for political reasons. The Rohinya crisis made investors nervous.

It's so frustrating to see a huge refugee camp in Burma on the border with Thailand. Here, many

Karen refugees have been living for over 50 years under horrendous circumstances, forgotten by the world.

An entrepreneur from Singapore, an American investor and a Karen general thought of developing ecotourism and agriculture in this area to create jobs for the refugees. After 2012 there was so much hope in Myanmar. The election of Aung San Suu Kyi gave hope to the citizens of Myanmar and the Karen, too, who hoped to get out of the camps and create a new life by developing their Karen state. I spent several days with the Karen leaders. At the time, they were hoping that they might be able to put down their weapons. But they were also very cautious because they had been lied to so many times by the central government.

One very charismatic leader and general was the initiator of the project. He set up an enterprise to develop the Karen state with the development funds from an American friend and an Australian entrepreneur who was the CEO of this company. They hired me to set up a similar project as our hotel and school in Bhutan.

I went to Mae Sot, a border town in Thailand,

and spent two months there to get to know the Karen
and the region before starting the project. Going to
the refugee camps and the base camp of the Karen
liberation army was like being in a war movie. The
refugee camps are huge, about 100,000 people have
been living in them for over 50 years. As far as the
eye could see, there were thatched huts with very
poor people in them. I was thinking that this must be
hell during the rainy season when everything turns
to mud. The refugees are not allowed to construct
buildings out of concrete or other durable materials
because the Thai government doesn't want them to
stay there permanently. But they have already been
there for half a century under appalling conditions. I
spoke to an Italian doctor who visits the camp every
year, and he told me that they have diseases from the
middle ages because of their primitive housing. There
was barbed wire around the camp, and we were not
allowed in. Children were peering at us through the
wire. Close to the camps on the river that divides
Thailand and Myanmar was the military basecamp
of the Karen general and his army.

When I visited the base camp in the jungle it felt

as if I had landed in a movie. I saw many young Karen fighters with machine guns in their hands. Most of them were short, sturdy jungle people, with dark skin and very friendly faces, some no older than 18. Like the Bhutanese, the Karen like to chew betel nut, so some of the young men had red teeth. Most of the solders wore T-Shirts with "Kaw Too Lei" printed on them, which means Free Karen State. The base camp was a clearing in the jungle at the river, a beautiful place but very primitive. Here, too, there were only bamboo buildings with thatched roofs. They also had electricity but that was all.

About 200 Karen with their families lived here. There was even a school where volunteers from America, Europe and Asia taught the kids. I learned that the Americans were from a Christian sect. I didn't like them very much, they weretoo dogmatic and narrow minded. In that environment and with the knowledge of what these Karen people were going through, it was heart breaking to see these rich Americans trying to convert them. No respect for the Karen tradition and religious systems. To me it looked like cultural and religious exploitation again.

The Karen people are the kindest and gentlest people I ever met, it's heart breaking when you hear the stories about all the terrible things the Myanmar government has done to them and all the other ethnic groups in Burma. To get an idea of the opportunities that existed there, the general took me deep into the Karen state to see the military headquarters. We drove in a convoy with a small army on four wheel drives with machineguns ready to shoot. Next to me in the car sat a young Karen girl with two handguns on her hip, she reminded me of Lara Croft.

I have so much respect for these people, so much respect for the general who dedicated his life to the protection of his people, to fight for over 50 years already against that brutal Tatmadaw, the Myanmar military.

It is good to know that the Karen people finance their purchase of weapons through the sale of teak wood. These Karen are not involved with the drug trade. Other groups in Burma are.

During my stay in Mae Sot, the Thai border town, I had a Skype call with an American organisation that claimed to support a project to help refugees.

We wanted to set up a hotel and hotel school in Myawaddy, an expanding town in Karen State close to the border with Thailand. The idea was to absorb the young people from the refugee camps and train them in hospitality so that they could earn a living and someday even start their own hotels or guesthouses. The tourism sector in Myanmar is growing so fast, and there is a huge need for trained hotel staff.

This organisation was a fund financed by George Soros to help refugees to get out of the camps and start a new life. This was the project we worked on for the Karen people. I had a talk with nice Indian lady who understood what we were doing and it seemed she approved. She said she would call me back. After four weeks with no news I decided to call her.

"Well," she said, "I like your project very much and I see how important it is, but we cannot support you because our team of experts for Myanmar are in Yangon. We have no team in Myawaddy, so we cannot support projects in that area!"

"But the refugees are at the border with Thailand," I said, "not in Yangon! What is that team doing in Yangon? Everybody know that all the refugees in

Burma, all the Kachin, Karen, Wa, and Shan are at the borders of neighbouring countries and most of them close to Thailand."

Of course she was sorry that she could not help us further, etc.

These people should be ashamed of themselves. I wish I could detain all the billionaires of the world for one month in a camp like the one in Karen state and take away all their money and privileges.

Again, I learned that if you are close to decision makers in big philanthropic organisations you can be sure of their support. If you are not an insider, you can forget it.

We had so much hope to start the project in Karen State, but apparently we were too hopeful. The investors withdrew because of political uncertainty. The Karen people gave up hope. Besides, they never trusted the Myanmar government to begin with.

SELF REFLECTION OF AN INVETERATE LOVER

Last year we handed over the hotel school to Mr. Jigme. He built a new dorm for 75 students and the school is now 100% in the hands of Bhutanese people. This was the goal of our foundation right from the start and we achieved it. The Western hotel trainers did an excellent job training the locals. The restaurant was doing well and was nominated by the Lonely Planet as the best restaurant in Bhutan. Now a famous worldwide TV channel wants to make a documentary about the hotel school with me. We have to be quite creative here because, of course, I cannot get into the country.

I must admit that I am very proud of what we accomplished with very little money. The international development organisations throw millions at projects in emerging markets and most of them fail. Our small but very effective project has already trained about 250 students in less than three years and helped them all to find jobs. That is absolutely amazing, both compared to others and just on its own terms. Maybe this was the reason that they blacklisted me? Were we just too successful? Did I perhaps disrupt the social order?

So, several years on, I'm still blacklisted. I ask myself was I too naïve? Or, would I have done this project even if I had known what I was getting myself into? I hear from many people, investors and entrepreneurs who are working in emerging economies, that my story is just one of many. It seems that what happened to me is almost a template for what often happens. Emerging markets in general and Bhutan in particular like to get the investments but don't want the foreigners to see what they do with them. Some Bhutanese contacts told me: "They want your money but not you." 'They' being the royal family because they have all the assets of the country in their hands.

I am a woman who grew up in the 1970s and 80s. I was a political activist and always wanted to help to create a better world. This was one of the reasons I studied social anthropology and non-Western sociology. It was always my mission to help others, especially the poor of this world.

I worked in Bhutan because I love the country and its people, and there was so much to do. Now I realise that every country has its own fate and must walk its own path. Now I see it is better not to intervene. I come from such a different world, with a completely different value system. Most of all I cherish my freedom. If I have to pay the price of losing my freedom and my freedom of speech, then for me that price is too high. I am not willing to do that.

At first I was embarrassed to tell people that I was blacklisted in Bhutan. Strangely, people who have been travelling and working in developing countries seemed to understand my situation and told me that they were not surprised. In their experience, things like this happen frequently to people who create something good. Often the elite in a country feels threatened and doesn't want what you want. Therefore, they don't want you.

Blacklisted in Bhutan?

Many people have told me to be proud of it. I have been asked to speak at conferences around the world about my experience and, the result is that my story helps to spread the word that this country is not the Shangri La and happiest country on the planet.

My love for Bhutan is still there.

Of course it is.

How can I not love the villages and villagers, the caring culture among the ordinary people, the rich history and spirituality, the mountains and rivers, the temples, the spicy food and even the crazy pigs?

I feel a deep love for all the amazing people I met in Bhutan. They will be in my heart forever.

But now I want to tell my story, and to share my experiences all around the world.

Bhutan is a country like any other.

And that, perhaps, is the best thing I can say about it.

ABOUT BHUTANESE NAMES

Bhutanese people have in general no family names many names are the same for female or male. The meaning of names are in general religious or linked to the village where they come from. E.g Karma Wangdi, this can be a female or male name. Karma stand for the Karma Kargyu school of Buddhism and Wangdi is a town.